"I went back to South Africa hoping against hope to find some evidence that the dam of apartheid was ready to crack. I went where few whites ever go, and saw the forces mounting to tear down the wall of separation and oppression. I also talked with whites and listened to their visions for a white South Africa and realized that the government has not allowed cracks in the dam, rather, it is meticulously reinforcing the dam to ensure the longevity of apartheid."

FOREWORD BY JOHN PERKINS

APARTHEID

TRAGEDY IN BLACK & WHITE

GORDON D. AESCHLIMAN

Regal Books
A Division of GL Publications
Ventura, California, U.S.A.

Rights for publishing this book in other languages are contracted by Gospel Literature International (GLINT) foundation. GLINT also provides technical help for the adaptation, translation, and publishing of Bible study resources and books in scores of languages worldwide. For further information, contact GLINT, Post Office Box 488, Rosemead, California, 91770, U.S.A., or the publisher.

Published by Regal Books
A Division of GL Publications
Ventura, California 93006
Printed in the U.S.A.

Library of Congress Cataloging in Publication Data

Aeschliman, Gordon D., 1957-
   Apartheid: tragedy in black and white.

   Bibliography: p.
   1. Apartheid—South Africa. 2. Race relations—Religious aspects—Christianity. 3. South Africa—Race relations. I. Title.
DT763.5.A64   1986   305.8'00968   86-20339
ISBN 0-8307-1178-3

1 2 3 4 5 6 7 8 9 / 91 90 89 88 87 86

REPUBLIC OF SOUTH
AFRICA

Pretoria
Johannesburg !
Soweto

Cape Town

AFRICA

illustration by Dawn Benley

Contents

Foreword   9

Love Labor   11

 1 Home Again at Midnight   13

 2 Battle of Blood River   27

 3 Color Me White   33

 4 Black Gold, White Power   45

 5 Double-talk   57

 6 No Land's Man   71

 7 "A Brutal Jesus"   79

 8 No Connections   87

 9 Heavenly Minded   93

10 Paying the Bills   99

11 Cosmetic Changes   109

12 Communists in My Backyard   117

13 Savages   125

14 Wilderness Voices   133

15 Uncle Sam   143

16 Cross Roads   151

17 Dayspring   159

Appendix 1
  The Freedom Charter   161

Appendix 2
  Resources and Opportunities   169

Foreword

Gordon Aeschliman's book, *Apartheid: Tragedy in Black and White,* is a very moving account of a very tragic and most difficult situation. Yet, despite all of the sadness and pain it caused me to read it, there exists a ray of hope, and of course, that hope lies in the authentic gospel of Jesus Christ.

The sadness I see lies in the fact that we as Protestant evangelicals, and, more particularly, as white Christians, have not been able to see the gospel as being more powerful than race and economic interests. It's unfortunate that basically the only confrontation to Western Capitalistic Imperialism has been communism. Because the Church has so sided with monopoly and big business and, in the process, has not held itself accountable, it makes godless communism seem the only option for the oppressed.

The whole story that Gordon presents here reminds me of my growing-up years in America's deep South. The story he tells, in terms of what is happening to the blacks in South Africa, is really how I remember my whole life in Mississippi. And the same arguments that the Dutch

Reformed Church uses in South Africa to justify oppression are all the same arguments I heard in Mississippi as I grew up there and during the '60s.

The ray of hope lies, of course, in the gospel, which is neither black nor white, and as it is lived out in the lives of those emerging leaders of both races, mainly Bishop Desmond Tutu, Alan Boesak, David Bosch and Nico Smith, and many others I do not personally know. It's their denouncement of violence and their acceptance of personal suffering that might really be preparing South Africa for the future, and, as Gordon points out in this book, many of them will probably never see the future effects of the lives they are presently living.

I pray that God will open the blinded eyes of that wicked government so that South Africa can avoid the kind of blood bath that took place in Hitler's Germany and Amin's Uganda. We need to pray for all of those people who are suffering from and fighting against apartheid. And, pray also that their lives will inspire a whole new generation of both blacks and whites to join together to make South Africa a nation where all can enjoy the prosperity God would have for all people.

Love Labor

Sherrie's an unusual sort. Raised a shy country girl in the high desert area of California, she married a jungle-born kid from Zululand, South Africa who spent most of his life in the fast-paced big city of Johannesburg.

It would have been more than enough support had Sherrie simply *tolerated* me while I was writing this book, but she did much more. She listened carefully to the endless recountings of my boyhood days. She laughed at me when I screamed my head off at newscasters and big-time American TV evangelists who had all the solutions for my country but couldn't even pronounce President Botha's name correctly.

Sherrie encouraged me to return to South Africa in preparation for this book, leaving her to hold down the fort in California with three kids under five years old. Most importantly, she held unswervingly to the biblical mandate to "do justly and love mercy" as our comfort in the face of rejection by close friends who thought we may have gone off the deep end.

Maria Leydon has been my research assistant for several months as I finished the book. Her help has been invaluable and, in my opinion, a direct labor of love for the oppressed in South Africa. She celebrated the completion of the manuscript by running off and marrying one of my best buddies from college days, Doug Henderson. Best wishes you two—always keep Jesus at the center.

1
Home Again at Midnight

The 747 eased off Nairobi's runway and gently rolled its gigantic body till it pointed south. Its graceful gliding made mockery of my stomach, which instantly began to churn and bubble like a witch's brew gone wrong. Next stop: Johannesburg, South Africa.

Only four hours remained between me and Jan Smuts Airport. My mind quickly rehearsed all the turmoil listed in the latest headlines:

"14 Killed in widening strife"—police had fired into a group of rioters.

"Bomb kills 6 in shopping area"—no one had claimed responsibility.

"Unrest spreads to homelands"—blacks burned two other blacks alive.

"Police whips drive singing youths from shopping center"—300 school children singing *We Are the World* were dispersed for violating internal security regulations. At least 30 were treated for cuts left by police whips.

"South Africa city cracks down on Christmas"—police banned Christmas caroling by nonwhites as "emotional" and required them to apply for "political rally" permits to hold their Christmas candlelight services.

"Am I crazy to be on this plane?" I asked myself. I left the United States in a frenzied rush just a few days after the South African government gave me the "go ahead." They had given my entry visa request the cold shoulder for several months, and I assumed I wouldn't be allowed in. The day my visa arrived, Dan Rather announced on the evening news that all journalists were now being denied entry to South Africa. Being a member of that newly defamed profession I decided to get to South Africa before my visa would be revoked.

Jan Smuts Airport reeled in the airplane like a big fish on a hook, and I realized that South Africa was doing the same to my heart. Ten years ago, I left South Africa bearing a passport with an official stamp on it declaring: "Deprived of South African citizenship." That was a white lie to be sure, because I had actually *renounced* my citizenship. But as the plane made contact, I discovered an important principle: I had left South Africa, but South Africa had never left me.

"God, I love this country," escaped from my lips as I deplaned and worked my way across the tarmac to the terminal building. Drawing in a deep breath, I savored the familiar humid air of the summer afternoon. "Yes, this is home," I told myself.

My passport lists my nationality as American, and California has been my second home for a decade now. Some people who grow up in one culture and then move to another never feel completely comfortable in either place. They say they're only at home in the air, traveling between their two homes. But that's not my experience; my home never left me.

It's strange to love something you hate, but I can't help it. I deplore South Africa's legalized racism and the havoc it wreaks on black families. I get angry listening to whites who twist reality and force a sword between the races. But it *is* home.

I guess among other things, it's my love for South Africa that makes me hate its injustices. Many mornings I've picked up the newspaper, hoping to read that the government has decided to abandon its system of oppression. Sometimes I've cheered the petty changes in the laws, believing that the dam of apartheid is beginning to crack, and all its laws are about to crumble under the pressure of the people's demand for freedom.

I went back to South Africa hoping against hope to find some evidence that the dam was ready to crack. I went where few whites ever go, and saw the forces mounting to tear down the wall of separation and oppression. I also talked with whites and listened to their visions for a white South Africa and realized that the government has not allowed cracks in the dam; rather, it is meticulously reinforcing the dam to ensure the longevity of apartheid.

The more I talked with both blacks and whites, the more convinced I became that only an explosion could dismantle that wall. The explosion seemed inevitable, and the time was drawing near.

My first day back in South Africa, I went to Soweto.

This large township of 2 million blacks is just half an hour outside of Johannesburg, and its residents fill most of the grunt labor needs of Johannesburg's white citizens. Its African-sounding name (to foreign ears) is actually a government abbreviation for SOuth WEst TOwnship.

A friend of mine, Caesar Molebatsi, pastors the Ebenezer Bible Church there, and I called him to see if we could spend the day together. It was Sunday, so I enjoyed a typical service of hearty black singing, laughing and fiery preaching. Caesar bounced up and down the center aisle of the room, rented from a government school building, beaming with delight in his role as unpaid pastor.

One of his legs is wooden, a daily reminder to Caesar of the ills of South Africa. Hit by a white driver, Caesar had to listen incredulously to the judge who sympathized with the driver's need to hit a black pedestrian instead of the curb—the curb could have damaged his car. And besides, Caesar no doubt was in a white area without "due cause."

An embittered teenager, crippled for life and with a self-esteem a little lower than a car fender, Caesar decided to kill the driver, knowing that it would mean the death penalty for him. He watched the driver's daily patterns and one day, confident of his kill, a gun in his jacket, he went to settle the score. The only hitch was that on the way, he met one of those obnoxious street-witnessing Christians who lack sophisticated skills in evangelism. Asked the simple question, "What will happen to you if you die tonight?" Caesar instead settled his score with God, and has been working for Him ever since.

Caesar, his wife Chumi and I ate lunch that afternoon in a white restaurant in white-inhabited Roodepoort. I told the restaurant owner that I was an American tourist and wanted to take my black friends to lunch. He obliged and escorted us to a far, secluded corner.

We laughed a lot over old familiar jokes about the government, but inside I doubled over from the pain of looking on at a friend who suffered the calamity of having the wrong color skin. Only three miles from this restaurant was the home of half my South African boyhood. The place brought back pleasant memories of mulberry fights, bicycle races, carnivals and hikes through the nearby hills. We lived in a large house planted on a fruit tree-dotted yard, a house with an ever-present Mom, warm hearty meals and long hot baths on cold winter nights.

Caesar's skin barred him from such boyhood memories. "It's unfair," came the obvious thought as I stared across the table at my brother and friend. I admired Caesar and wondered what my life would be like had I been born with his skin.

After lunch we drove to Daniel Moalusi's house in Soweto. Daniel is a member of Caesar's church. He and his wife, five children and ailing mother live in a two-bedroom house—the whole thing isn't much bigger than a single-car garage. The bathroom is a covered hole in the ground. The government built this house—specially designed for blacks—and Daniel rents it from them for $60 each month.

We squeezed sideways through the little space left in the kitchen between the stove, refrigerator and table, worked our way through the living room—a room not much larger than my bathroom back home—where a dozen or so women from Ebenezer Church were meeting for prayer, and stepped into a bedroom that doubled as the dining room.

Sipping some tea and eating some freshly baked biscuits that I knew he couldn't afford to give me, Daniel told me about his life. Even though his pay has never exceeded $120 per month, it does help meet some of his expenses. When employed, Daniel spends most of his time away from his family, working long hours and traveling three or four hours each day to and from work by bus and by foot. But his jobs never quite provide enough for a square meal for the whole family each day. When his children get sick, he can't afford $10 to take them to a doctor, so he just hopes that they get better by themselves.

Between jobs, Daniel was arrested for being in white areas without "due cause." The police demanded to see the permit that would allow him into the white city of Johannesburg. Blacks must be employed to have such a permit. When he tried to explain he was looking for a job, the police retorted, "That's your problem. You're breaking the law."

He was arrested and convicted after a railroaded trial. His family had to fend for themselves during his six-month prison sentence and the additional three-month "probation" period, when the government "sold" his labor to a white farmer for 12 cents a day.

Two years ago Daniel was out of work again. He stole some clothes from a shopping center with the intent of selling them on the black market. "My five children were hungry—they had been without food for four days. I had to do something," he explained. He was caught, but before being sentenced to a year in prison and a six-month probation, he was released on bail. That night he hitched a ride home. Thinking of how to break the news to his wife, and picturing the suffering his family would endure with no income for the next year and a half, Daniel told his story to the driver.

The driver was a member of Ebenezer Bible Church.

Caesar and the church took care of Daniel's family while he was in prison, stretching their meager income to pay the rent and feed an additional seven mouths. When probation time arrived, Caesar found a white Christian farmer and persuaded him to hire Daniel for the six months and even to pay him a wage. Daniel is still employed by the white farmer, and his whole family now enjoys a personal relationship with Christ, thanks to the ministry of Ebenezer Bible Church.

Being black is a hardship. Being black and Christian is a trial. Caesar is well acquainted with what it means to suffer for the sake of Christ. He's been arrested several times, without charges, simply because he's a leader in the black community. Police regularly intimidate him just to keep him "in line." The last time they arrested him, they told him, "We have a wheelbarrow full on you." In other words, "Cause trouble once, and we'll put you away for good."

Police intimidation isn't all. Caesar finds himself under fire from both sides. Black activists in Soweto also monitor his movements. Police informers are the worst enemy of these radicals, so Caesar has to limit his contact with whites to avoid accusations of collaborating. Before my visit, it had been three months since he'd taken a white into Soweto with him.

Last year, Caesar planned a Christmas trip for 300 youths to a church camp retreat. Black activists in Soweto had proclaimed Christmas a time of black mourning, and they confronted Caesar for violating it with a "celebration." They threatened his life "to make an example" of him to discourage others from resisting their cause.

Caesar met with the leadership of these radicals to see if they would be willing to compromise or negotiate. What stunned him the most was that the leadership was comprised of people Caesar knew as committed Christians. "All of them were former evangelical leaders," Caesar told me. "They became disgruntled with white hardness of heart and gave up. They're working for freedom and justice, and white Christians are calling them terrorists or liberals. So that's what they've finally become."

Caesar is empathetic toward those leaders. He too has felt the rejection of white Christian leaders who don't understand his pleas for them to use their political rights to demand justice. Often they reject him as "uppity" or "revolutionary" or "not grateful for what the whites have done for blacks."

"The church has to be the solution," Caesar told me. But black Christians don't find it easy. The rising tide of anger in the black community has led many to reject Christianity.

Daniel Madi, who works with Caesar in Soweto, tells of the difficulties he faces in communicating the gospel with his peers. "People wonder how the white God can also love blacks. Youth are rejecting their parents' religion, saying that it has put their minds to sleep, makes them docile. To them religion has become part of the enemy.

"Some of them ask me, 'Why does God make the white man successful only to stand on my neck?' I don't have a good answer for that." Daniel told me he wonders about that question himself.

For blacks, Christianity is associated with the white government that oppresses. Black Christian leaders are becoming much more open in condemning the government. Increasingly, they're rejecting the option of negotiation with the government because, in their terms, "You don't negotiate with the devil."

At the end of 1985, more than 100 black Christian leaders signed the *Kairos Document,* a statement of their
belief that reconciliation with the government is impossible. Part of the 25-page document reads:

> We can imagine a private quarrel between two
> people or two groups whose differences are
> based upon misunderstandings. In such cases it
> would be appropriate to talk and negotiate to
> sort out the misunderstandings and to reconcile
> the two sides. But there are other conflicts in
> which one side is right and the other wrong.
> There are conflicts where one side is a fully
> armed and violent oppressor while the other
> side is defenceless and oppressed. There are
> conflicts that can only be described as the
> struggle between justice and injustice, good and
> evil, God and the devil. To speak of reconciling
> these two is not only a mistaken application of
> the Christian idea of reconciliation, it is a total
> betrayal of all that Christian faith has ever
> meant. Nowhere in the Bible or in Christian tra-
> dition has it ever been suggested that we ought
> to try to reconcile good and evil, God and the
> devil. We are supposed to do away with evil,
> injustice, oppression and sin—not to come to
> terms with it. We are supposed to oppose, con-
> front and reject the devil and not try to sup with
> the devil.
>   In our situation in South Africa today it
> would be totally unChristian to plead for recon-
> ciliation and peace before the present injustices
> have been removed. Any such plea plays into

the hands of the oppressor by trying to persuade those of us who are oppressed to accept our oppression and to become reconciled to the intolerable crimes that are committed against us. That is not Christian reconciliation, it is sin. It is asking us to become accomplices in our oppression, to become servants of the devil. No reconciliation is possible in South Africa *without justice.*

Bishop Desmond Tutu, 1984 Nobel laureate, has been a voice for nonviolent change in some of the toughest situations. He's seen the suffering violence brings into people's lives, and he risks his own to prevent it.

I met Tutu in his little office behind the main Anglican church in Johannesburg. It was hardly the sort of setting you'd expect for the bishop of South Africa's leading city. The afternoon rain beat against his window, sending trickles down the inside wall. Watermarks betrayed what must have been a regular occurrence. A harmonica lay on his cluttered desk. Tutu played a short tune on it, unable to conceal his delight that it was a gift from Stevie Wonder.

Tutu's humble office illustrates the simplicity of his call. "We are told to live for others. The Bible commands two things: 'Love the Lord your God with all your heart,' and 'love your neighbor as yourself.'"[1] Those aren't cheap words for Tutu.

A couple of days after I spoke with him, Tutu rushed to nearby black township, Alexandra, to quiet a crowd of 30,000 angry blacks. They were protesting the deaths of youths shot by police during a riot. Police had put the death toll at 19; community leaders put it as high as 80.

Tutu pleaded with the crowd to disperse quietly and not to kill. His life has teeter-tottered many times in this balance of black anguish and rage. Fortunately, that day they heeded his request again.

The structures of white oppression have also threatened Tutu's life. Several times when government officials have sent in bulldozers to raze black settlements in white areas, Tutu has stood in front of them with Bible in hand.

Nineteen eighty-five was the worst year for black people in the history of South Africa. Outbreaks of violent protest by blacks began in late 1983, when a new Constitution again denied any black political rights. More than 1,000 blacks died by police bullets, and a state of emergency lasting more than a year gave police of any rank power to arrest and detain anyone without any charges. (The state of emergency was lifted in March 1986, but all powers given to police during the state of emergency have been transferred to them as normal powers—the state of emergency continues, as what passes for "normal" in South Africa.) Also during 1985, the white military moved into black areas on full-time surveillance while the government tried to keep journalists and photographers out of black areas.

As much as Tutu pleads for nonviolence, it is still difficult for blacks to believe South Africa's strife will be resolved any other way. In a poll recently conducted by the London-based *Sunday Times,* 69 percent of the blacks interviewed said South Africa's problems would be resolved by a civil war, although only 43 percent felt violence was justified.

It's a despairing picture. But as Tutu said to me, "We always believe the night is nearly over." He's not alone in this uncanny ability to hope in the face of oppression and constant defeat.

Rev. Allan Hendrickse, leader of the colored Labor Party, put it to me this way: "Our Christian duty is to live in hope. When the night is darkest, that means the Morning Star is about to appear."

Chief Minister Buthelezi, leader of the 6 million Zulu South Africans told me: "I'm very despondent but can never abandon hope. I continue to work. God will not abandon us, we are His children."

The signers of the *Kairos Document* have hope. The concluding paragraph reads:

> There is hope. There is hope for all of us. But the road to that hope is going to be very hard and very painful. The conflict and the struggle will have to intensify in the months and years ahead because there is no other way to remove the injustice and oppression. But God is with us. We can only learn to become the instruments of *his* peace even unto death. We must participate in the cross of Christ if we are to have the hope of participating in his resurrection.

The night is nearly over for these blacks. Dawn is coming, they believe; the struggle itself is a sign of hope. The darker the moment, the sooner the light.

Most of the whites I chatted with in hotel lobbies, churches, corner cafés and airplanes saw the night differently. They don't see the coming dawn. They feel the clock stops at midnight. They fear that midnight means bloody revolution, and they fear that the clock will strike very soon.

Bounding over the back hills of Zululand in a four-wheel drive, Graham Beggs spoke to me about midnight. Graham comes from one of South Africa's most affluent communities, Hilton, a quiet resort village not far from Zululand. While working for the forestry department of the government, Graham found himself drawn away from the security of his life into trusting God to use him as a servant to blacks in KwaZulu.

"When I think of the night, I think of Peter," Graham said, maneuvering the truck around ruts and rocks. "Think of the night he endured in agony, crying bitterly having denied Jesus.[2] That is our night here. The church has denied Jesus Christ, but it will soon recognize the grief it has caused God."

Graham was speaking from his own life. "The night is nearly over; the light is coming."

———

One night after I returned from South Africa, I watched the clock strike midnight. I poured myself a cup of tea, pulled back the living-room curtains, sat back and waited for the dawn.

Slowly but surely the light chased away the darkness. Chickens next door competed with birds on the other side of the house as they squealed in delight at the coming day. Some dogs began to bark, and soon I was listening to a neighborhood choir affirming its love of the light.

My mind drifted to a favorite passage in Romans 13: "'Love your neighbor as yourself.' Love does no harm to its neighbor. Therefore love is the fulfillment of the law

. . . . understanding the present time. The hour has come for you to wake up from your slumber . . . . The night is nearly over; the day is almost here."³

For a moment I was back in South Africa, walking familiar ghetto streets, chatting with well-meaning whites in city restaurants, listening to government officials tie themselves in knots with complicated rationales for their wrongdoing and laughing with Caesar when I really should have been crying.

I reminded myself that South Africa's struggle is not against Marxists, black terrorists or white liberals. Its greatest enemy may be the Church which claims to be Christian, but may be nothing more than a whitewashed tombstone.

"It's midnight back home," I thought to myself. "But it doesn't have to be."

Notes
1. Matthew 22:37,39.
2. See Luke 22:62.
3. Romans 13:9-12.

2
Battle of Blood River

White South Africa began at the Cape, where a sleepy settlement had grown up as a halfway point for Dutch trading ships shuttling goods between the Far East and Europe. The Cape was a refreshment station, where a few Dutch settlers provided fresh water, meat and vegetables for the sailors.

When England took control of the Dutch colony in 1806 in order to preserve their shipping interests, South Africa experienced its second cultural dynamic—the clash between English and Dutch settlers. (The Dutch, of course, had already confronted the Africans: One tribe, known as Bushmen, were nearly exterminated; another, the Hottentots, were enslaved.).

Unlike the passive Dutch farmers at the Cape, the British had grand visions for Africa. They weren't content to let the Cape remain a sleepy shipping station. Britain's imperialistic dreams, fueled by the occupation of the Cape, eventually led to an all-out scramble northward. Cecil John Rhodes (after whom Rhodesia—now Zimbabwe—was named) led the way; his goal: an English-dominated Africa literally stretching from the Cape to Cairo.

The British outlawed slavery in 1833, and that may
have been the only good thing they ever did for South
Africa. In fact, their expansionist goals and ill treatment of
the Afrikaners may have been one of the most significant
factors in the formation of today's intransigent, Afrikaner-
ruled South Africa.

The Dutch—or Afrikaners as they came to be called—
wanted no part of either British agenda. They were hardy
individualists who had already survived for more than a
century on foreign soil and didn't want to be told how to
run their lives or rule their workers. In 1836, they set out
from the Cape by the thousands, striking into the interior
of the country on the "Great Trek." Like the pioneers of
the American West, they were looking for elbow room, for
open, unhindered living.

Instead they encountered the nomadic Xhosa tribe as
it moved southward. Caught between the British and the
Xhosa, the Afrikaners for the first time thought of themselves as "a people." When pursued by aggressive blacks,
the Afrikaners drew their ox wagons into large circles
called "laagers." Women, children and oxen huddled in the
center while the men fought off attackers on the perime-
ter. The laager became the symbol of their plight and
marked the beginning of their transition from individuals
pursuing freedom to a people struggling for survival.
When they managed to settle briefly without black attacks,
the British extended their legislative arm to include their
new-found territories.

The Trek was an arduous affair. Death, fear, sickness
and harsh physical conditions drove these unlearned Afrikaners to depend on the little biblical knowledge they had
acquired in the Cape. They found comfort and encouragement in recalling the Old Testament stories of God giving

overwhelming victories to the Israelites as they entered Canaan, the Promised Land. Itinerant preachers overcome by the hardships of the trekkers called them to be strong in God's strength.

December 16, 1838, marked a decisive date in Afrikaner history. A band of about 500 trekkers had encountered the Zulus, the strongest tribe in Southern Africa. Only weeks before, the Zulus had killed several Afrikaners in another wagon train, including their leader, Piet Retief.

Wagons drawn into a semicircle with a river completing the laager, the Afrikaners surveyed the grim view of several thousand Zulus taking positions in the fields surrounding their laager. Though they were vastly outnumbered, the odds weren't entirely against the trekkers. The Zulus possessed spears; the trekkers' armory included guns, swords and an old cannon, affectionately referred to as "Gertjie." The fresh memory of the recent slaughter, however, and the sight of the hoards of waiting Zulus convinced them that they required God's intervention.

So they made a covenant with God. It may not have been any different than a prayer I might pray when a strange noise in an airplane reminds me of the distance to the ground. But this covenant became the watershed of Afrikaner national pride and paved the way for the most holy of national observances.

History has it that Sarel Cilliers stood on Gertjie, Bible in hand, and led his people in a prayer asking God to give them the battle as He had so many times for the children of Israel as they fought for their Promised Land:

> Almighty God, at this dark moment we stand
> before you, promising that if you protect us and
> deliver the enemy into our hands, we shall for-

ever live in obedience to your divine law. If you
enable us to triumph, we shall observe this day
as an anniversary in each year, a day of thanksgiving and remembrance, even for all our pos-
terity. And if anyone sees difficulty in this, let
him retire from the battlefield.

The next day when the battle was all over, thousands
of Zulu warriors lay dead, and all the Afrikaners survived.
So many Zulus were shot while swimming across the river
toward the laager that the river turned red with blood.
The trekker's prayer was answered. The Battle of Blood
River, as they later named it, became the promise of God's
blessing on their modern Canaan, the Republic of South
Africa.

The Afrikaners launched into the next several decades
determined to establish themselves in this land of milk and
honey. They founded three republics in the eastern part of
the country. They also discovered rich diamond fields and
gold mines—the promise of prosperity as well as independence.

The lure of these riches, as well as their own imperial-
ist ambitions led the British to annex the Afrikaner republics. The Boer War, the Afrikaner's attempt to fight free of
British domination, completely overshadows the dimensions of the Battle of Blood River. From 1899 to 1902, the
Afrikaners were again a people struggling for survival.
Their laager mentality was tragically reinforced by the
war.

Soldiers expect to die in battle, but they don't expect
the same for their wives and children. The battle against
British soldiers not only left 3,000 Afrikaner men dead on

the battlefield, but also 26,000 women and children dead in concentration camps.

The anguish of this tragedy bound the Afrikaners together in a fashion that no victory, no matter how great, could have done for them. The laager mentality of a people struggling for their survival in the midst of an enemy bent on exterminating them (as they saw it) fueled the passion to conquer Canaan and usher in God's promised land.

What had been a messy theology at best became a unified biblical worldview which formed the bedrock for developments leading to modern-day South Africa. When the Afrikaner Nationalist Party finally won political control of the country in 1948, they quickly enacted a legal system that would ensure their God-given rulership over the land. Apartheid, as they called their ideology, kept the races separate, and the blacks subservient to white whims.

What started as an accident, a collision of races, became cemented into the nefarious legal system of the Republic of South Africa. But the Afrikaners still rule from the laager. Like wagons in a laager, the walls set up by apartheid laws and reinforced by a sophisticated military apparatus protect them from the outside world—a world they believe not much different from thousands of Zulus waiting to destroy them in their innocent quest for survival.

But inside that laager is no desperate huddle of men and women wondering if they will see tomorrow. Their innocence has given way to indulgence. There's a carnival going on inside those laager walls, a carnival created by the government and religiously endorsed as the birthright of every white citizen.

3
Color Me White

When I was eight, I joined a dozen American evangelical missionaries who were building a Bible School just outside of Johannesburg. This was to be a training institute to help coloreds get grounded in biblical truths and acquire tools for ministry.

Sitting far away in one little corner of the expansive piece of property was an overturned car with no windows or doors. Inside lived a black family with all their belongings. A few weeks before, one of these missionaries had told the head of the "home" to move, because this property belonged to the mission agency. After a second request with no results, it was "time for someone to make a decision."

I still remember the numbness and disbelief that lodged in my head as I watched these missionary men go into action. The black family was out for the day, but their belongings remained in the car.

With the same sort of spirit you find among a group of men moving a washing machine, these people hoisted the car onto a flatbed truck. They joked and laughed as they hauled the "junk" off to an abandoned mine shaft a hundred yards away. Home, belongings, all of it, went down.

Back at the foundation work at the school, they continued to lay the next round of bricks as though nothing significant had just occurred.

"What happens to them when they return tonight?" I inquired. It was difficult to imagine what sort of circumstances forced a family to live in such squalor. Desperation drove me to continue questioning as I pictured a black boy my age having to sleep in the tall grass that night with no "roof" from the rains that the gathering clouds were promising.

The men knowingly shook their heads and smiled at me with reassurances that "this is the best way to handle things."

Like little robots stamped out of a government factory, these men obediently performed according to the code for white South Africans. Considering most of them had been in the country for only a decade, they responded remarkably well. They made perfect citizens. That night they said prayers around their tables, set with plenty of food to reward them for the day's labor. Their utterances were nothing less than blasphemy.

I suppose there was a malfunction in my upbringing, because I never was able to understand what made apartheid acceptable. I wondered about that displaced black family on the Bible School property. What if by some freak accident of nature I had been born with black skin? Of course, since both of my parents were white (American missionaries), the odds were definitely stacked against me.

My birthplace was Zululand, home of the 6 million Zulus living in South Africa—they were all black. The sexual unions of mothers and fathers in that region automatically produced beasts no more deserving of respect than a cow used for plowing the field, or a pig raised to supply bacon. Unless, of course, it was white skin touching white skin during those intimate moments. In that case, the little jungle hospital in Ingwavuma, Zululand presented beautiful little boys like me who were deserving of all the tenderness, opportunities and goodwill a nation could afford its citizens. And more than that, it put at their disposal slaves who could easily be told apart from their masters by the color of their skin.

The duty of the South African government was to color my mind white, to impose on me a way of thinking, a way of seeing reality that would accept the blacks as backward—plagued by tribal rivalries, so childlike that they were dependent on the guidance and benevolence of a Big White Brother. And I was to be taught that the horrors done by me, a white, were actually "for their benefit" and sealed with the blessings of God Almighty Himself.

The idea of making sure South Africans were correctly classified by color had its origins in the period following the Boer War.

Jan Christiaan Smuts led the Afrikaner nation heroically in battle against the British during the Boer War. Fueled with a vision of God's promised land, he continued to lead flash strikes against British installations even after his nation surrendered. When he finally raised the white flag, he asserted his faith in God's great purposes for the Afrikaner people: "Perhaps it is His will," Smuts declared, "to lead our nation through defeat . . . to the glory of a nobler future, to the light of a brighter day."

That "brighter day" would come when Afrikaners ruled South Africa, unhindered by any other race or nationality. Turning again to their Bibles, they sought out a plan for their country. They saw that God instructed Israel to remain unblemished by other nations. If God instituted walls of racial separation, who were they to tear them down? Just as Israel would be degraded by the infiltration of non-Jews, so would the Afrikaner by mixing with the blacks.

Even though they lost the war and remained British subjects, Afrikaners dominated the politics of the Union. Smuts, in fact, became Prime Minister in 1939. As Prime Minister, Smuts articulated the political ideology that has shaped contemporary South Africa. In those days it was known as "The Color Question."

Smuts asserted, "The whole basis of our political system in South Africa rests on inequality." Blacks should not and could not be treated the same as whites or served by the same institutions, Smuts argued. To do so "instead of lifting up the black, degraded the white." He advocated the idea of separate areas where blacks would live and govern themselves, while whites lived in their own areas, and ruled themselves "according to the accepted European principle."

The color question was a religious as well as political issue, with clergymen and politicians together hammering out their beliefs about racial purity and white destiny. The *Broederbond* (Brotherhood), became a central forum for such discussions. The Broederbond was a secret society of Afrikaner leaders—including most of the top clergy of the Dutch Reformed Church—committed to establishing white supremacy.

Broederbond leaders found a certain fellowship in the

racial theories of Adolph Hitler. In 1941, Dr. Piet Meyer, chairman of the Broederbond, foresaw victory for the German race in Europe, and in that victory, the coming of racial purity and national pride.

Only seven years later the Nationalist Party, the party of the Broederbond, came to power and began to enact laws to separate the races forever and ensure the purity and dominance of whites. They have ruled without interruption since 1948.

With apartheid written into law, the Afrikaner wedding of God and country was consummated.

Reverend Nico Smith used to be a member of the Broederbond. He is one of the few Afrikaners in South Africa today who has been freed from the color white.

When I talked with Nico in his home in Pretoria, he was still reeling from the events of the previous day in nearby Mamelodi, a government-created town of 250,000 blacks. Nico had conducted the funeral of a 20-year-old black activist who couldn't take the pressures of the struggle anymore and committed suicide. After the funeral, the crowd of 5,000 mourners turned on a black police informer they had discovered. Nico convinced blacks not to kill a black police informant.

They had already bound the man's hands and feet and doused his body with kerosene. All that was left in this ceremonial killing was the "necklace"—a car tire placed around the victim's neck before his body was set on fire.

Endangering his own life in the middle of this angry mob, Nico convinced them to try the man in their own "people's court." Being the only white among them, the symbol of their oppression, the more natural deed would have been to kill *him*. But Nico was winning his way into these people's hearts after four years of serving many of them as a pastor.

Nico showed me a balsa wood model of a house he was about to build. Just that morning the government had given him permission to be the only white to live in a black township. Mamelodi would soon see its first white resident.

Nico was raised white. "I can still remember one of my earliest impressions was of my mother telling me that you just don't talk to a black person unless you want to give him an order.

"In my own house, as in most Afrikaner houses today," Nico went on, "blacks working in our homes had a separate tin plate and tin utensils. In our house those were put on a shelf deep down in one of the kitchen cupboards. Sometimes, I remember, while we were playing around as kids, crawling into one of the shelves and I accidentally touched those plates, a sibling would run to my mother and say, 'Niki touched those plates and cups!' My mother would tell me, 'Go wash your hands immediately! Don't go near there.'"

The first time Nico was confronted with the possibility of eating with blacks was after he had completed his theological studies and five years in the pastorate. He went to a conference at a German-run mission base and lunch was set for all attending, including some black pastors and evangelists.

"I couldn't sit down. I had a psychological block," Nico said. The missionary's wife laid a separate table for Nico in the study. "I sat there all by myself, having my meal all alone."

Nico was convinced these people just didn't know any

better. This sort of social mixing could lead to mixed marriages, "at which point you lose your identity, your God-given identity," according to all that Nico had been taught. Back then he thought that one had to *protect* that identity. It was obvious to Nico that these missionaries didn't understand what blacks really were.

As sure as he was about his views of white superiority, doubts began to arise because he realized that these were fellow black Christians.

When Nico was in his late 40s, he visited a black township for the first time. Disease, death, malnutrition, unsanitary conditions and overcrowding made for a squalor that he could never have imagined. Shocked by the suffering he encountered, Nico began to wonder if the God of Abraham really meant for blacks to live in such dehumanizing conditions.

Few whites in South Africa—less than one percent—have ever been to a black township. In fact, that's the genius of apartheid: It keeps blacks and whites in two separate worlds. A tourist or visiting evangelist can spend a week in South Africa and think that the country is the same thriving, modern, prosperous land that Nico knew before he allowed himself to see the conditions of blacks.

The physical layout of the "black spots" protect innocent white eyes from the plight of blacks. Black townships are hidden in the hills; the highways that take white commuters from their suburban homes to the major cities don't pass through places like Mamelodi. Ordinary citizens, and even sincere, mature Christians, never know the hurts their life-styles inflict on blacks as long as they live normal lives and stay on main roads—heeding the government propaganda that warns about the unpredictable, dangerous nature of black townships.

When Nico first saw this reality he had to go back to his Bible and ask some tough questions. In 1963, he had traveled to Europe and met Karl Barth, one of Protestant-ism's leading theologians, who had also led one of the resistance movements against Hitler's racist ambitions for Germany.

At the end of their conversation, Barth startled Nico by asking him if he felt free to preach the gospel in South Africa. Nico recounted their conversation.

"Barth asked me, 'Do you feel free to say whatever the gospel may tell you to say?'

"I said, 'Yes, I think I'm free.' At that time I really thought I was.

"'It is not that easy just to say yes,' Barth responded. 'Will you be willing to preach the gospel if you are con-vinced that the gospel is saying things your friends and community wouldn't like you to preach?'

"'I don't experience it that way,' I told him. 'I don't know how I'll react if I get in that situation.'

"'It's even more serious than that,' Barth cautioned. 'Will you be willing to proclaim the gospel if the govern-ment in your country says you may not proclaim that understanding of the gospel?'

"'I can't think that the government in my country would ever do a thing like that,' I responded."

Returning to South Africa, Nico slowly began to see that the government had colored him white. His preaching began to change, and after a few sessions with deacons who felt he needed "counsel," Nico was defrocked from the Dutch Reformed Church—the denomination to which nearly every Afrikaner belongs.

The right to preach was granted to those who believed in the Afrikaner dream. Nico resigned from the Broederbond. "I really got liberated," Nico told me. "I really began to preach the gospel."

Four years ago, Nico left one of the most prestigious positions a person can hold in South Africa, that of a university professor. He accepted the call to pastor a small black church in Mamelodi.

Nico is learning about a world that the government hopes few—in its scheme of separation—will ever discover.

The "things" that used to be house servants are suddenly becoming people to Nico. Whereas he used to see people that you "give orders to," he now has friends who live in two-bedroom houses—shared with as many as 15 to 25 other people. These friends wish their children could get an education, but school fees and books are too expensive. Their wages are too low for everyone in the family to eat every day; sickness and starvation are the norm.

Impoverished and powerless, they're caught in a dilemma: "The blacks are very afraid to say anything against the whites about injustices they experience," Nico told me. "I try to make them aware of the fact that they have the responsibility to because so many white people will say, 'You know blacks are quite happy; they're really very thankful that we whites are here to supply jobs for them.' What the whites don't understand is that the black people will almost never tell a white man, 'Listen, I can't live on this, you're paying me too little,' because they might be fired, and then they'd have no job at all. So they always try to say the things they know the white people want them to say."

Nico was approached recently by a white friend seeking advice because his servant had died on the job. This man confided that he didn't know the woman's last name, where she lived or whether she had any relatives. She had worked for this man for 20 years. Someone's mom just never came home again; someone's wife disappeared without a trace; someone's daughter got thrown out, just like an old iron that quits.

My time with Nico had to end abruptly because of a meeting he needed to attend. Last November women from Mamelodi peacefully marched to the mayor's office to protest the raise in rent. Their monthly income averaged $115 and rent had been raised from $45 to $85. As the crowd of 50,000 women approached the administrative building, police threw tear gas canisters into the front of the crowd and briefly opened fire on them, dispersing them rapidly back to their homes. Fifteen women and children lay dead on the ground. Three months later Nico was still battling with government officials to reduce the rent to its earlier level.

> Woe to him who piles up stolen goods and makes himself wealthy by extortion! How long must this go on?
> Will not your debtors suddenly arise? Will they not wake up and make you tremble? Then you will become their victim.
> Because you have plundered many nations, the peoples who are left will plunder you.
> For you have shed man's blood; you have destroyed lands and cities and everyone in them.
> Woe to him who builds his realm by unjust gain

to set his nest on high, to escape the
clutches of ruin!
You have plotted the ruin of many peoples,
shaming your own house and forfeiting
your life.
The stones of the wall will cry out, and the
beams of the woodwork will echo it.
Woe to him who builds a city with bloodshed and
establishes a town by crime![1]

It had been over 10 years since I stood at the base of
the awesome, five-story high Voortrekker monument,
only minutes from Mamelodi. This passage of Scripture
came to my mind as I thought about the significance of this
beast stretching toward heaven.

Just as the Israelites were often instructed to build an
altar after winning a battle so that children could be
reminded of the Lord's hand in their victories, a century
after the Battle of Blood River Afrikaners built the
Voortrekker monument to keep the covenant they had
made with the Lord to "observe a day of thanksgiving and
remembrance." They had "built a city with bloodshed,"
created a nation "by unjust gain" and now they built this
altar to invoke God's blessing on their deeds.

The lowest floor in the monument is a gigantic circular
room with an altar smack in the middle of it. Chiseled into
the rock on top are the Afrikaans words, *Ons vir jou Suid-
Afrika,* meaning, "We are yours South Africa." Precisely
at noon on December 16 a small beam of light from the sun
finds its way through a specially prepared hole at the top of
the monument. It casts its ray down in a perfect circle on
the altar, illuminating the solemn pledge.

This is the "holy of holies." This is the temple of the

God of South African whites. This is the mecca to which the nation's faithful make their pilgrimage to renew their love and commitment, to purify their hearts, to keep themselves white. And only whites are permitted to enter this temple.

A fresco inside the monument depicts the major battles the Afrikaners had to fight in their march to the promised land. The circular wall surrounding the monument is made up of wagons, reminding the nation of South Africa's struggle, reinforcing the laager mentality and in essence barring outsiders from the nation of white Afrikaners who fought with their lives, first to survive and then finally to build the new Israel.

My mind flashed back to the first church the Afrikaners ever built in Cape Town. The "Mother Church," as the Afrikaners call it, is filled with replicas from the original worshippers. I visited the church shortly after it had been refurbished. They had rededicated the church and the pastor had read the prayer that Solomon had prayed when the temple of Israel was dedicated. I sat in one of the pews, opened my Bible to 1 Kings 8 and tried to picture the preacher booming out some of the incriminating words nestled in the middle of that prayer: "When a man wrongs his neighbor . . . . Judge between your servants, condemning the guilty and bringing down on his own head what he has done."[2]

I couldn't help but wonder how God was going to answer that prayer.

Notes
1. Habakkuk 2:6-12.
2. 1 Kings 8:31,32.

4
Black Gold, White Power

A tourist magazine was waiting in my hotel room the night I arrived in South Africa. In it was my invitation to the city's 100th anniversary celebration. The letter from the mayor boasted that Johannesburg, "mere grazeland for cattle" a hundred years ago, had become the "pacemaker of the sub-continent," built by the "hard work and dedication of our citizens." He invited me to enjoy all "this wonderful City of Gold" had to offer.

There was a lot to enjoy. The rest of the magazine's pages were filled with invitations to exclusive restaurants and nightclubs, advertisements for furs, diamonds, gold and other expensive jewelry and a listing of special tours that could show me the city built by the "hard work and dedication" of its "citizens."

With one exception, all the blacks appearing in the ads were doing the work—serving the tables, pouring drinks, servicing cars and pushing canoes through the swamp safari.

Whites were doing the dining, dancing, drinking and laughing, decked out in jewelry and furs—enjoying. I went to bed thinking that South Africa is white, the South Africa, that is, that one enjoys. The blacks are there, a labor pool 21 million strong, only to ensure that whites enjoy themselves.

Early the next morning, I left my downtown hotel room to walk through the streets and watch the blacks pour in from surrounding townships. Government-run trains and buses spat out hundreds of thousands of scurrying laborers who were rushing to get to work on time. It was 5 A.M. Most of them had been in transit from their homes for more than an hour—many for as much as three hours. One bus had an advertisement painted all across its side, "Next Stop Happiness." None of the blacks inside seemed all that excited.

At 6:30, returning to my hotel room, I encountered three blacks raising the South African flag outside a large bank. "My name's Harry Kennedy," boasted one of them when I told him I was a journalist. "Tell your friends in America that we're all one people here—the whites tell us what to do, and we do it."

Feigning ignorance about the second flag they were hoisting, which displayed the symbol of Johannesburg's 100th anniversary, I asked, "What's that?"

"Oh, haven't you heard?" asked Harry. "Johannesburg is celebrating its 100th anniversary."

"When will it be?" I returned.

"I don't know." A glint appeared in his eyes. "They haven't invited me to the party."

Harry knew his role in South Africa. An uneasy feeling gripped the air as we glanced across the street at a bus unloading whites on their way to work. An advertisement on it for a placement firm boldly announced, "We place you first."

The Afrikaners had a dream for a white South Africa, a vision of a race pure and beautiful, a sanctuary for the worship of God who obviously favored them highly, second only to Israel.

They got much more than they bargained for.

South Africa is the most mineral-rich nation in the world, and its white citizens enjoy one of the world's most comfortable life-styles. Its mines yield more than 50 percent of the world's gold, 70 percent of its diamonds and 80 percent of its uranium, platinum and chromium. Countries like the United States pay millions of dollars each year for South African minerals because of their critical importance to the military and to the aerospace industry.

But South Africa's most valuable resource is its black population—slaves in essence. This seemingly endless supply of cheap labor makes a dream come true for 4.5 million whites in their haven flowing with milk and honey.

The supreme irony of the white view of South Africa is that the most valuable resource, absolutely essential to the prosperity of the country, is a constant source of problems. Whites view South Africa as a white country, where blacks are aliens who have wandered into their pure domain. Yet they can't afford to remove all of the blacks: the goal of apartheid is to create wealth and ensure whites its maximum, exclusive benefits. Control and exploitation of black labor is inseparably linked to that end.

Sarah Gertrude Millin, a South African novelist, described the whites' dilemma in telling terms:

> The white man has awakened the native, and,
> like a dream, the old savage life is ended. He

has been called. He has arisen. He is on the road—travelling in the shadow of the white man, carrying his chattels . . . The white man looks around at this being he has himself aroused, who is following him; who is serving him; who is dependent on him; for whom, on the journey he must provide. And he thinks how useful it is that someone else's back shall be bowed under his burden, while he is free to exult in the air and sun of Africa.

The native follows patiently. Now it is time to take food. The white man throws the native a scrap. They go on again. The native is useful to the white man, but also he makes demands on the white man's resources. The master begins to wonder, a little resentfully, if he would not, on the whole, have been happier without his servant . . . The journey is an arduous one. The white man opens up again his bundle of food, and thinks that, really, he cannot afford to give any more away, that he needs it all himself. He begins to be resentfully conscious of this creature who makes demands on him. If only he could shake him off, he mutters to himself. He begins to feel that he is being dogged. He begins to suspect that the native isn't keeping a decent distance. He begins to distrust him, to fear him. The native, he knows, is not getting enough to eat. What if he were suddenly to take it into his head to spring upon him, and rob him of his means of subsistence, and run away ahead of him, and leave him there to starve?

How can he get rid of the native? How can

he get rid of him? . . . He begins to make suggestions to the native that he should retrace his steps, return home to his beginnings. "Look here," he says, "this journey of ours has been a mistake. You and I can't do it together." . . . "It is hard for both of us," admits the native . . . "You'd better leave me," says the white man. "You'd better go back home . . . . "

"Go back?" says the native. "Home? . . . But the road has fallen in behind us. And my home is broken up. How can I go home now?" . . . "You are taking the bread out of my mouth," protests the white man . . . "But I am carrying your load . . . " "I could carry it myself. It would have been better . . . " "Then why did you call me?" . . . They face one another, unable to move forward, unable to move back . . . And, "I wish to God I never had called you" mutters the white man.[1]

The Nationalist Party came into power offering the fulfillment of God's promises to the Afrikaners, yet even they accepted the fact that the black was a permanent part of South Africa. Their plan was to remove as many blacks as possible from the white regions, especially the cities, and isolate those who remain in "black spots."

The key to the plan is the "homelands." Pursuing the age-old strategy of divide and conquer, whites drew up a list of 10 African tribes (although most anthropologists argue that there are really only three major tribes with many subtribes). To each of these tribes, it assigned territory, allegedly representing the original home of the tribe.

In actuality, these pieces of land represent mountains, desert and other landscapes that whites don't want or can't use. Blacks represent 73 percent of South Africa's population, yet in the homeland scheme they are granted only 13 percent of its land. More horrifying still, the more than 10 million blacks who live in the homelands have less than two percent of the nation's arable land.

"Take away a man's money and he'll find a way to go on. Take away his home and you take away his reason for living." Those were the words Prime Minister Vorster used to tell his Afrikaner constituency what a good thing they were doing in creating the homelands. The irony of the statement lies in the fact that so many black homes have been bulldozed to make the white dream of independent black homelands a reality. Since 1960, the government has forcibly—and often violently—removed 3.5 million blacks from "white" South Africa to these desolate and impoverished homelands.

In 1979, the Riekert Commission was appointed to improve "manpower utilization"; its report summarized the logic of the system:

> The first and foremost point of policy is . . . that every black person in South Africa, wherever he may find himself, is a member of his specific nation [homeland] . . . . The second [is that] the Bantu [African] in the white area, whether they were born here or whether they were allowed to come here under our control laws, are here for the labour they are being allowed to perform . . . . The third principle . . . is that the fundamental citizenship rights may only be enjoyed by a Bantu person within his own eth-

nic homeland . . . . The fourth policy point . . .
is that the maximum number of people must be
present in their own homeland.

The homelands offer a neat solution for those con-
cerned about the democratic reputation of South Africa.
Denied all political rights in South Africa, the blacks are
deemed "citizens" of the homelands. According to the
plan, each homeland will have an opportunity to become
"independent" and elect its own government. Four homelands have accepted this dubious honor, though no other
nation in the world recognizes their independence.

Since the South African government does not keep
statistics on the citizens of these independent homelands,
it can turn a blind eye to their poverty. A Carnegie Foundation study in 1985 concluded that 9 million homeland
residents are living *beneath* subsistence level. Families in
the homelands live on an average of $30 per month.

For the 10 million blacks who live in "white" South
Africa, the structures of control on their lives are nothing
less than repressive. To keep blacks out of the urban
areas, South Africa has established a policy of "influx control." Blacks can only travel to and live in white areas with
permission, evidenced by a stamp in the identification document, or "life book," they must carry at all times.

Blacks with permission to work in the white areas are
confined to black townships—government-created slums.
A black can't go into the white city to look for a job unless
he has the proper permit, which he can only get by having
a job. More than 140,000 black men were imprisoned in
1985 for violating the country's pass laws.

Hundreds of thousands of black workers live in all-male
dormitories, separated from their families back in the

homeland for 10 or 11 months of the year. Their wives and children are, according to the government, "superfluous appendages" who shouldn't be allowed to take up room in white South Africa.

While severely restricting the flow of people from the homelands to the cities, the government is aggressively enforcing migration in the other direction. Inevitably the "unproductive" people are the first to be shipped out: the aged, unfit, widows and women with young children. The only blacks who are exempt are those who have permanent residency—a status that can be achieved only after working for the same employer for 10 years.

Since blacks in South Africa are only worth their labor, the services offered to them are deliberately substandard. Former Prime Minister Verwoerd introduced the Bantu Education Act in 1953, saying, "What is the use of teaching a Bantu child mathematics when it cannot use it in practice? . . . Education must train and teach people in accordance with their opportunities in life."

Threatened by the fact that education, especially that provided by churches and missionaries, was leading blacks to "seek greener pastures," the Afrikaner government clamped down on education. They eliminated any integrated schools that may have existed, and took away from South Africa's churches the right to teach blacks in private institutions through high-school level. The churches were given deadlines to sell their properties or demonstrate that they had found alternative uses for them.

The public education system spends $700 each year for a white student and only $57 for a black student. Black classrooms are overcrowded, led by undereducated teachers and ill-equipped with even such basics as chalk. Students have to purchase their school materials, which most of their families can't afford. Only two percent of blacks make it through high school and pass the nationwide college entrance exam. Eighty-two percent of the blacks get less than five years of schooling in total.

Even these repressive measures of control have not been enough to satisfy the whites in their laager. Increasingly isolated on a continent dominated by independent black governments, South Africa has continually sought to suppress any hint of dissension from within or without. The prime label they apply to any suspected "enemy" of their regime is communist.

In 1950, the Suppression of Communism Act defined the intolerable ideology as "any doctrine or scheme which aims at bringing about any political, industrial, social or economic change in South Africa by the promotion of disturbance or disorder, by unlawful acts or omissions, which aims at the encouragement of feelings of hostility between black and white."

It's been a convenient law for South Africa's government because just about anything or anyone upsetting the apartheid applecart can be considered "communist."

But the government hasn't slowed in the generation of its control laws. Blacks and other dissidents are regularly detained without trial or legal counsel, confined to their house and removed to another area. Dangerous public figures are "banned," which means they cannot make political statements in public, be quoted in the press or meet with more than a few people at a time. Others have their passports withdrawn. Religious gatherings are also subject to control. "Law and order" is the phrase that practically rules the nation. The police are excused from almost any deed when they cry that "law and order were threatened."

Keeping the system in place requires power—the power of a tremendous military and police force. The budget of the South African Defense Force increased nearly 1,000 percent under P.W. Botha's leadership as Defense Minister from 1964 to 1978. In the same period the number of conscripts grew and the age range of potential recruits increased significantly. Botha, now president of South Africa, has continued to act on his conviction that international threat, internal unrest and the decolonization of nearby states require an overall aggressive military strategy to secure South Africa's future.

At age 16, a little letter addressed to me presented itself with a foreboding official stamp. Inside a note read: "Report to Pilgrim's Rest October 19, 1975 for training in the South African Defense Force."

The date was nearly two years away, but standing with the draft card in my hand, my mind pictured U.S. B-52 bombers ripping apart territories in Southeast Asia. I didn't understand the war, but I knew that although thousands of U.S. soldiers were being killed and being replaced, others were burning their cards, burning their flags and demonstrating against the Vietnam War.

I was just a South African kid being told to learn how to defend my country, and I felt caught in a dilemma: Supposedly this was God's country and as the white government leaders were careful to state, He had given them the duty of running it. But on the other hand, "God doesn't do things the way the South African government does," I told myself.

The only rationale I'd have to report to "Pilgrim's

Rest" for my military training would be to learn how to protect South African white interests—which hurt the black. Romans 13 says: "Love does no harm to its neighbor."[2] Being assigned to two years of border duty to shoot at blacks who were hoping for a more just South Africa for millions of slaves didn't seem too biblical.

"It's unfair," I thought, "that I should have to make such a decision." Complying with the order meant doing things I couldn't justify as a Christian; it meant betraying the truth I'd come to know about the South African system; it meant possibly pointing a gun to the heads of many of the black youth my parents had let become my friends.

Jail was an alternative, but not that pretty of a one for a 16-year-old who had heard the horror stories of what police do to black prisoners and "kaffir lovers" (black sympathizers).

I wrote the government and requested they exempt me from military duty. The reply was reassignment to a different training camp. My mind entertained the possibility that this was a specially created training facility for young men who required an unusual amount of guidance in the colorization process.

I decided on a different alternative. Renouncing my citizenship was not easy to do, but it seemed the only good thing to do. I had the luxury of dual citizenship and therefore did not face the uncertain future of a political exile. The police officer who signed me away to the United States communicated his emotion quite clearly with steel-cold stares, and the U.S. consulate finalized it by faithfully recording the government's words, "Deprived of South African citizenship."

Out in our backyard, huddled by the door to our servant's quarters, which my parents never used for that purpose, I lit a match to the draft cards and held them as long as I could—even letting them burn my fingers a little. Maybe it was a child's need to experience *some* punishment for a clumsy decision.

The sensation was unfamiliar, but somehow I felt, "This is what growing up means"—making a decision that seems right in the face of uncertain consequences.

The flame flickered in the Cape wind and gave way to a trail of smoke. My color left me at that moment. I bent over and cried that my country wouldn't.

Notes
1. Sarah Gertrude Millin, *The People of South Africa* (Alfred A. Knopf, Inc., 1954).
2. Romans 13:10.

5
Double-talk

Sitting inside C.P. Rencken's office this year brought back all the emotions of sitting in the principal's office as a schoolchild. Intimidation and punishment were the two pillars of the educational system and, as I was to realize later, the pillars of the government power over its citizens.

The line was clearly drawn on my very first day in first grade: Punishment is immediate for anyone breaking the rules. The palms of my hands collided with the teacher's angry yardstick before noon that day. It was all very simple—she told me to sit next to a girl I didn't like. During recess I relocated, and hence the hand-spanking.

(That's the closest I ever got to an arrest for locating myself in an area not designated for me. Probably that very day at least several hundred blacks were arrested in nearby Johannesburg for venturing into white areas.)

Somehow a stubborn streak had weaved itself into my personality by age five, and that encounter with my first grade teacher was a challenge. Visits to the principal's office where canings on the rear end were meant to correct my social deviance became a part of my weekly routine. Every visit was a terrible experience as I watched the principal select a stick from his armory and order me to bend over. The pain was intense, but the pleasure of showing off the stripes drawn on my tender skin from the whipping outweighed the price.

The real pleasure was the feeling inside that those teachers were "never going to win." The school system was designed after the regimented British system where all students wore uniforms, cut their hair to prescribed shortness, stood when addressing teachers, marched in straight lines between classes and jumped to attention whenever the principal appeared.

It's probably to my father's blame (or credit) that everything in me resisted this kind of treatment. Hours of listening to him trade stories with his peers concerning government control and his own boyhood days of mischief set me up for repeated violations. I was constantly stepping across the disciplinary line. I cut school, slid down the banisters, locked teachers in closets, pirated the intercom system to dismiss school, removed desks from classrooms during the middle of the night and groaned instead of laughed at my teachers' stupid jokes.

There was one line, however, that I never ventured to cross—criticizing the government of our country in a classroom discussion. The fear the system fed into my mind was more than a match for my rebellious streak. Stories of what happened to political prisoners left me convinced that political dissension was not child's play.

No specific law stated that citizens could not have their own opinions, but the Communism Act, denying the right to hold a "doctrine" that led to "encouragement of feelings of hostility," left very broad parameters for the government to clamp down on nonconforming citizens. My tenth grade teacher almost lost her job and qualification to teach in any government school because she allowed one of my peers to vent his feelings on government control. The principal overheard the short discussion on the two-way intercom system and immediately called her to the office for a formal reprimand. Her personality virtually changed for the remainder of the school year; our childlike minds could only imagine the threats that had brought about the transformation.

Rencken is, in a sense, a principal. His title is Chief Information Officer of the ruling Nationalist Party and his job involves controlling the information that goes to his constituency as well as quelling any party voices that might dissent on government views.

Sitting across from him in the parliamentary office building was no comfortable feeling, especially since I had chosen not to disclose my South African origin.

"I'm an American citizen and would like to know the real story about your country," I offered. "What should I tell my friends back in the United States about the government's policies—you know we read about unrest all the time."

I was nervous that he might discover my background during our conversation, and I actually feared the consequences. The most he could do, of course, was put me on an airplane back to the United States. But my childhood experiences of sitting across from a "government authority" prompted irrational thoughts in my mind (wasn't there some obscure law which would exempt me from U.S. protection in this particular instance?). "Former South African Imprisoned for Life" flashed the imaginary newspaper headlines as I wondered if I should just wet my pants as an excuse to get out of his office. The thought that I may wet them involuntarily, however, led me to decline a second cup of tea.

"We don't have any unrest in this country," Rencken responded to my first question. "There are a few things happening in some isolated spots, but the country is stable."

That very week more than 200,000 blacks in three instances had protested brutal treatment by police and the response they received was tear gas, shots fired into crowds, police cordons and deaths. What Rencken really meant was, "Where the whites live, that 16 percent of the population that makes up the *real* South Africa, there is no unrest." And of course the whites have no reason to riot.

For an hour and a half I dutifully tape-recorded all the "official line" of the Nationalist Party. The government has a well-developed talent for saying things as they are not, and this session was certainly no exception. Part of the success of apartheid has been the government's ability to simply say things that are not true, but in such a way that the outside world believes it.

In fact, I was fortunate enough to observe the wide gulf that lies between what the government portrays as truth for the benefit of those outside South Africa and the facts as they are given to its citizens. Shortly before I arrived in South Africa, foreign minister "Pik" Botha offered in a press conference that South Africa might someday have a black president. He was immediately reprimanded by the President for "suggesting new policies for the ruling party." When I asked Rencken if it were possible that South Africa might have a black president, his response was, "We have not yet discussed that in the Party."

Just then the phone rang, and he launched into a conversation in Afrikaans over the same issue. I remembered more than enough Afrikaans from my school days to be able to enjoy the inside line that Rencken spat over the phone in no uncertain terms. "It's ridiculous to think we'll have a black president. That goes against our party stance, and is simply not an option."

Just before I left for South Africa, President Botha outlined, in what was billed as a history-making speech, fundamental changes in apartheid: "Apartheid is an outdated concept," he said. "We believe that human dignity, life, liberty and property of all must be protected, regardless of color, race, creed or religion." He said reforms were forthcoming.

In South Africa I heard the official interpretations of that speech for South African audiences. Education Minister F. DeKlerk said he "would never let blacks into white public schools as long as the current government is in power." In less than a week after Botha's "historical" speech, white South Africans were also reassured that race classification would remain and blacks would have to continue living in black areas in substandard conditions.

Among the outsiders duped by the government's truth for external consumption was the Reagan Administration, which praised Botha's commitment to end apartheid. U.S. Ambassador Designate J. Douglas Holladay told me, "There's a real reformist wing in the Nationalist Party . . . . Change is coming internally . . . a force that is really promoting change."

The language of reform abounds in South Africa, and a good deal of it is simply double-talk. Whites point with pride at all the "major" changes in the structures of apartheid that have been enacted over the past few years—the repeal of the mixed marriages act, desegregations of

beaches, the election of colored and Indian houses of parliament. The real impact of any of these changes on the
miserable lives of blacks is debatable at best. The more I
listened to the waves of double-talk that came out of the
mouths of South African politicians, the more convinced I
became that they are changing their rhetoric, but have no
intention of releasing their hold on the power and prosperity of the country.

Columnist Otto Krause articulated the steps forward in
this noble battle in a December 1985, editorial:

> There is apartheid and apartheid and apartheid.
> The word is as loaded with emotion as with dif-
> ferent meanings, given who you are.
>
> There is apartheid in its early form of lega-
> lised discrimination, coupled to white *baasskap*
> [lordship]—48-style segregation.
>
> Then there is apartheid in its latter style,
> and more valid form of separate development—
> of tidying up the map of South Africa and putting
> cultural groups together in their own indepen-
> dent countries, just as the Europeans did, at the
> cost of many wars.
>
> Finally, there is apartheid according to our
> enemies, meaning any sin they wish to attribute
> to those fascist, racist whites in South Africa.
>
> The word apartheid remains on the books,
> whereas manifestly it should be discarded in
> national interest . . . by declaring roundly that
> apartheid is no longer Government policy.
>
> That word not only does South Africa
> immense harm in the world, but also bedevils
> relations within this land . . . .

Most of all, apartheid's two original meanings are increasingly irrelevant. Government is dropping legalised discrimination; and separate development is being swung around.

The only meaning of apartheid that remains is the ugly one, as determined by our enemies, who make it what they want. We should not afford them that advantage. Our ship should avoid that semantic iceberg.[1]

Botha's speech promised that the government would stay away from the iceberg labeled "apartheid," but his administration threatens to break the ship apart completely on icebergs of political double-talk.

The government boldly states that it is against "the political domination by one community of any other." What they mean is that blacks will never be allowed to dominate whites. They say they don't exclude any group from the political process, but the only way blacks can participate is through the voices of a few "representatives" of the black community who are handpicked by the government.

The minister for Constitutional Development and Planning said in early 1986 that power sharing among all the groups was "a necessary ingredient of democracy." But he just as quickly ruled out the hint of one-man-one-vote because, "minority groups [meaning whites] would have no opportunity ever to become the majority. They would be permanently relegated to a position of subordination." [Never mind that it's always been that way for blacks.]

He also boldly proclaimed: "We reject any form of discrimination, be it on the grounds of race, culture, religion or sex. Human dignity must be advanced and any affront to it eliminated." In 1985 alone, 1,000 people deemed to be threatening human dignity were "eliminated" by police bullets—and they all happened to be black.

When the government speaks of "equal rights" it is referring to preserving the already grossly unequal privileges of whites, meaning whites have the right not to change their current life-style in accordance with black demands or needs. The South African government, for all its public horn tooting of its achievements toward a just society where there is no discrimination on the basis of race, has absolutely no plans for an integrated society. The 1983 South African Annual, published by the government, quite simply states, "a common society for whites and nonwhites is unacceptable to the vast majority of white South Africans."

Nowhere is the double-talk more unpalatable as when the whites talk about what they have done to improve the lot of the blacks. Botha told the world last year, "No white minority government anywhere in the world has done more to raise the standards of living of black communities as we did in South Africa over the years. We are a Christian people, we know our job, and we know our duty."

Rencken may have been a little less optimistic, but he assured me, "We have yet to see blacks die of starvation in South Africa."

I asked him why there was such a high infant mortality rate for black infants, while white children have one of the lowest death rates in the world. "Those deaths occur because of peculiar black patterns," he replied. "Mothers are giving their infants black tea instead of milk. This leads to all the symptoms of malnutrition and resulting deaths. It's not a question of poverty." I didn't bother to point out the devastating effects on those families the government moves to the homelands: a quarter of all children under a year old die during these relocations, representing one of the world's highest infant mortality rates.

But the solution to the old Color Question—what to do with the blacks—has its most complete answer in the homelands policy. South Africa can boast of its "equal rights" policy by reasoning that whites have equal rights in white South Africa and blacks have their rights in the independent nations that have been given to them.

I asked Rencken if the blacks really wanted to live in these "nation states." He responded, "We don't force people to take independence; no one moves against their own will."

That very day, police had to quell unrest where the government decided to move 120,000 blacks into KwaNdebele, a "nation-state" that blacks, according to the government, really wanted. Chief Moutse vowed to defy the white government attempts and stated that his people would "resist to the last man."

Not far from where Rencken and I were talking was a "black spot" called Khayelitsha. More than 50,000 homes were built there recently by President Botha's administration, and blacks are being gathered from all over Cape Town to be settled in this one area. The first week that government vans arrived for the non-forced removal, police killed 18 blacks and wounded an additional 230 who were resisting the move.

The way the government talks about the homelands, they make it sound like whites probably would be happy with an integrated society, but "the truth is," the blacks don't want it. Blacks "have their own political and constitutional structures." Supposedly they're naturally given to nonintegration because of their distinct cultural preferences.

Even more disturbing than the government's double-talk is the way they twist the words and actions of black leaders to appear to support their policies. Chief Buthelezi, leader of the 6 million Zulus in South Africa, who has rejected the government's offer of independence for "KwaZulu," has been held up as a model of a black tribal leader. He is allowed to travel abroad as a spokesman for South African blacks. The government makes it look like he supports the homeland policy.

But Buthelezi told me that the homeland concept is the "most abhorrent system devised . . . . It's dehumanizing and denies that we're all created by God." When I asked him about the discrepancy between his beliefs and the way the government portrays him, he simply said, "I have never for one moment supported the homeland concept. We must immediately abandon color discrimination and independent homelands and demand universal suffrage."

He called the policy of separating black laborers from their families a "wicked system." Not far from Buthelezi's home live 1.5 million squatters who, in his words, "escaped the government homelands illegally because of economic hardships, and now live destitute and unemployed" in shacks made of "scrap metal and plastic."

But again, President Botha manages to say things as they are not: "I have the cooperation of the vast majority of black South Africans in this country." A *Sunday Times* poll conducted among blacks shortly after that statement showed a total of one percent of the black community listing Botha as the one "who would make the best President for South Africa."

Sun City is only a two-hour drive from the Voortrekker

monument. This Las Vegas-style resort on the border of Bophuthatswana, one of the "independent nations" created by the government, is the most prosperous homeland site. Legalized gambling, pornography and live naked ladies make this a favorite vacation spot for many white South Africans who don't have access to those outlawed attractions in the rest of the Republic. Saunas, golf courses, swimming pools, ritzy hotels and personal female escorts make up the rest of the package.

The borderline between white South Africa and sham-state Bophuthatswana is not clear. Several times the road dipped into "South Africa" and then back into "Bophuthatswana" as I sped across the countryside to interview some vacationing whites. Along the way I picked up several blacks who were walking along the side of the road. They were farmhands on Afrikaner farms for generations back, and, as I discovered, they knew little about the outside world.

Our conversations typically began with, "Hullo, I'm Gordon."

"Pleased to meet you, *baas* [boss], I am _____."

"I am visiting from the United States."

"I see *baas*, I am from Mr. _____'s farm."

Not one of them recognized the United States as being anything different from the farm down the road. One of them, Abraham, perked up when I said "California." He had "heard of that place."

A few miles outside of Sun City, I turned off the main road onto a dirt road leading up to one of the white farms. It was impossible to resist the temptation of meeting one of the farmers. The dirt road carved through an orange grove and spilled out at a beautiful house surrounded with green lawns, flowers and equipped with all the modern conveniences of any American home I've been in.

Helene, mother of the home, greeted the unfamiliar rental car driver who explained he was an American tourist on the way to Sun City, and "just wanted to meet a few friendly farmers in the neighborhood." True to a part of Afrikaner hospitality I grew up with and still love, she invited me in for a cup of boerekoffie (farmer coffee made mostly with hot milk) and rusks, a hard bread that gets dipped in the coffee. I felt completely at home, enjoying her gracious spirit and warmth that is associated with socializing among whites, feeling protected from the summer afternoon storm furiously pelting the windows with hail and listening to her expound white South Africa. She sat in a family heirloom chair that had belonged to some of the earliest trekkers.

"The government is being nice to the blacks by letting them have their own countries." She had read the propaganda well and believed every word of it. "We've always tried to be good to them," she continued.

As our conversation droned on above the noisy hail, my eyes drifted across her groves to the little mud huts that housed her servants. Helene's three young children were playfully chasing a pet bird through the house. It struck me that they knew a lot more about what "being good to them" meant than did the little black children huddled inside the one-room hut trying to stay dry.

Helene sincerely thought of the homelands as being "other black countries." The South African government paid her family to move from their old farm because it was inside the territory designated for Bophuthatswana. She had watched their old farm deteriorate under new leadership. This confirmed her belief that blacks are just not like whites.

"They lack culture," she told me. Helene teaches Afrikaans to black children in a government school. "They know nothing of England or classical music. It's as though the world only began 50 years ago."

But then of course they were never taught much more than how to cook and make tea for the white farmer, how to pick fruit and pack crates and how to do whatever the baas demanded because that is what blacks are supposed to do. If a white ever took an interest in history from their point of view, they would recount the evidence that over the generations skin color is what has always made the difference.

Our conversation ended with Helene showing me family pictures that dated back to the Boer War. Helene could have just mentioned they were "great grandpa and grandma," but the Boer War was just as much her history as her bloodline.

Sun City may as well have been the hotel center I was staying at back in Johannesburg. Blacks did the work; whites did the enjoying. The few exceptions made for some interesting conversations. Sanza and Jeremiah were up from Soweto and didn't find much comfort in this black nation.

"It would be good to live in your country," Sanza told me. "At least there you are treated like a complete person." Sanza had never been to the United States, but had seen the number one TV hit, "The Cosby Show." "You're just a nobody here," he confided. "People walk over you like a dog."

Duncan worked the bar. He was bitter after working here for four years, and was going to quit at the end of the month. "It's like a prison. I came here for freedom, but I'm spending my time making whites happy about my independent nation. They're the only people benefiting."

My mind flashed back to Rencken's office as I marveled how complete the government had been in setting up white South Africa. Even the limited attractions inside these so-called independent nations served the white wants.

I had played the devil's advocate with Rencken about the wisdom of setting up these homelands: "How can you expect Americans to invest in your country when you might give away part of it to blacks?" I jabbed. "Who wants their investments jeopardized by new little countries run by unstable black governments?"

"You don't understand the way things really are," Rencken returned. "Your investments in those homelands are critical to the future of South Africa. We would protect any of your money in those homelands."

"How?" was the obvious return.

"If those governments ever go toward a socialist form, we'll just have to replace them."

I kissed my tape recorder on the way down the elevator. I felt like a schoolboy who had just checkmated the principal.

Note
1. Otto Krause, *London Sunday Times,* Dec. 19, 1985.

6
No Land's Man

Our family moved to Goodwood during my senior year in school. A month later, we hired a truck to pick up the junk that had accumulated when we remodeled the backyard. The driver was a *colored*, and he quickly pointed out that he remembered this house from the days when he lived in Goodwood.

"The government moved us all out because they wanted Goodwood for the whites," he explained.

The house was never to feel like "home" to me after that conversation. My mind pictured lines of coloreds, with bags on their backs, climbing into trains and being hauled off to another government-prescribed living area. And then like a flock of vultures, whites came swooping in on Goodwood to settle in their new homes. "I'm a thief," I often used to think as I tried to visualize people of a different color walking down the streets.

Many of Goodwood's coloreds were shipped off to Bishop Lavis, a shantytown of 25,000, half an hour away. In the 20 years since they had to give up their homes—

"because this is white now"—little has been done to improve their lot. Some still have no running water or electricity, utilities that were part of their Goodwood homes.

Apartheid has never been able to clear up the messy problem of coloreds. Government statistics put their number at 2.6 million, as it has done for the past 15 years. They probably add up to as many as the whites—4 million.

Unlike blacks, whom the government can relegate to some distant parched mountain under the guise of an anthropological argument, the coloreds aren't that easily discarded. They arrived in the Cape approximately nine months after the Dutch settlers arrived—in the wombs of black women who had mixed with white men. White Afrikaners have tried at times to deny such behavior, but family trees have tied many of the most conservative whites to these earlier mixed parties.

The Afrikaner revulsion to white mixing with black was made clear in the Immorality Act of 1957. It forbade "unlawful carnal intercourse," which meant sex between whites on the one hand with a black, colored or Indian on the other. Not only was sex prohibited under this law, but also anything deemed "immoral or indecent." Kissing between whites and blacks is one such indecent act that has resulted in arrest. The Immorality Act followed one of the first laws introduced by the Nationalist Party after it came to power—the Prohibition of Mixed Marriages Act, which outlawed marriage of whites to members of any other racial group.

There is no land of origin for these coloreds except the bodies of blacks and whites. Usually their hair and features come out looking like they're white, but their skins are heavily tanned from day one. It's not easy for a racially pure government to decide what to do with such an animal, but some things are given: Put them all together in one area; keep decision-making privileges from them; and don't let them mix with whites on trains or buses, in restaurants, bathrooms, hotels or schools.

In 1983, the country adopted a new Constitution that established a tricameral parliamentary system. Besides the white parliament, a special House of Representatives was created for coloreds and a House of Delegates for Indians. (South Africa's 800,000 Indians are descendents of laborers shipped in to work on sugarcane fields. The government has lumped them into the colored living areas.)

Billed as a major step forward, the government represented the tricameral system as "true power sharing" in South Africa. What it didn't tell the world was that blacks were still altogether excluded and that the coloreds and Indians were given decision-making power only in dealing with their internal concerns—sewer lines, school buildings, etc. Whites maintained full power and veto, and no changes were to be made in the basic rules of racial discrimination.

Reactions to this announcement were mixed, but by and large the colored community rejected the idea as a sham. Some saw it as a step to improve their lot by entering into debate with the government on a regular basis, but most saw it as a slap in the face to the black and an insult to the colored by still keeping them out of the central decision making.

Dr. Allan Boesak, a colored South African and president of the World Alliance of Reformed Churches, opposed the step. He formed a political action group called the United Democratic Front (UDF) to oppose the tricameral concept, but the government persisted. Boesak mobilized his newly formed group to boycott the colored elections and rallied the support of more than 500 human-rights groups. The result was that only 18.2 percent of the colored population voted for the government initiative.

Nevertheless, the government declared the election a success and confirmed the appointment of members to both houses. Some serve as their people's "popularly chosen representative" even though they received less than a total of 300 votes.

Rev. Allan Hendrickse has chosen to participate in this government scheme, knowing he represents a minority view among coloreds, but has not budged in his sentiments about apartheid. Hendrickse told me he finds apartheid, "Evil, dehumanizing and destructive of self-worth." He says that all racially discriminatory laws should be abolished immediately because "Whether I'm originally a Pole, Jew or Zulu should have nothing to do with how I'm treated by other humans." He's hoping that proximity to the government will result in influence.

The week before I arrived in South Africa, President Botha had made his "historical" speech on racial reform. Newspaper ads sponsored by the government boasted: "We are committed to equal opportunity for all. Equal treatment. And equal justice."

Hendrickse is a member of the President's Council, as well as a leader in the House of Representatives. He took his party members to the government dining hall in the parliamentary building immediately following that speech to test the words. "Sorry, whites only" was the greeting. Hendrickse and his men staged a sit-in for an hour at the restaurant before peacefully leaving. His son Peter summed up their feelings: "We were treated like dirt, something filthy that was spoiling this lovely white restaurant."

Coloreds and Indians have a definite economic advantage over blacks. Their homes are fairly modern, their salaries significantly higher, and the laws that restrict freedom of movement for nonwhites apply less pressure to their routines of shopping, churchgoing and work. Some have suggested the government is hoping to pull coloreds and Indians into the "white" category to increase its power base against blacks, but nonetheless, they are rated and treated as low-class citizens, undeserving of the finer things of life that are meant for whites only.

———————

Basil Leonard, a colored friend of mine, described some of the ambiguities of a colored's life. He and his wife were hoping to buy a house recently and discovered as they looked through newspaper ads that property in colored areas was priced significantly higher than properties twice the size being sold to whites. And whites earn twice as much as coloreds.

Basil is teaching a church-growth class at an evangelical Bible School in Cape Town. The textbooks advocate home-cell groups as a means of church growth, but Basil finds the idea isn't always applicable to coloreds, because their houses can't accommodate groups. "Recently 19 of us turned up at a two-room house. We sat all over someone's bed, although most of us had to stand. It embarrasses the host," he told me.

Basil used to teach accounting, and he told me of the struggles of one promising student. "He never did his homework. Or even if he did it, it was not very well done.

So I called him in one day, and said, 'Look, Bell, what is the problem? Why aren't you doing your homework?' He wouldn't speak. So I said, 'Look, please, you've got to help me to help you. Tell me, what's the problem?'

"So it finally came out. 'We are twenty people in the house where I live,' he told me. 'And we have two bedrooms, and a lounge. There are always more than two or three people in a room. Always. I never have privacy so I can do my homework.'

"I said, 'Now you have done it a few times. Where have you done it?'

"He said, 'Well, I do it sitting on the toilet.'

"This is for accounting, which means he has the textbook, a ledger, a cash book, a journal. Every time someone wanted to come to the toilet, they would knock on the door, and he had to pick up all four books and get out. And then when they were done, he went back in. That's how he did it."

Alex, Basil's wife, also teaches. Last year she had an exceptional student in her class who told Alex at the beginning of the year, "I'm very sorry, I can't continue school."

"What do you mean, you can't?" Alex asked.

"Well my mom said I must rather go to work because there just isn't enough money coming in."

Children as young as 10 years old are being told by their parents, "Come now, you've had enough education. You must go work for a living."

Westerly, a colored township, has always stuck in my mind because one evening our family drove through its outskirts, and I saw a man hanging limp from the window of a third-floor apartment. I was 12 then. Whenever we drove by there after that, I looked at that window and wondered what happened to him. In a strange way he personalized for me the pain of colored people and put flesh around the graffiti painted on a wall near his apartment: "Born to die."

Late one night when I was 17, I decided to go to Westerly. Who knows why, maybe it was the need to meet someone and say, "I'm sorry for the hurt in your world." But 11 P.M. found me surrounded by a group of coloreds who weren't used to this sort of visit.

The conversation immediately launched into the abuses of the white government, and I had to agree with every accusation. I tried to separate myself from that guilt and explain that I was a Christian, believing that love does not harm its neighbor.

"But don't you read your Bible?" came the response. "It says to obey your government. Your God must be a white God to have put that sort of government over us."

What ensued was a rather unskilled attempt by me to explain Romans 13 in the context of what God expects governments to do. I failed hopelessly, but appealed to them to understand that not all whites supported the abuse.

"You'll never understand our suffering till you sleep in our beds," said Andrew.

"Then why don't you give me that opportunity?" was my response. They laughed at me, but I pressed the point. A half hour later I was walking alone with Andrew down a dark dirt road leading to his home.

My imagination raced with excitement as I anticipated the chance to be a little closer to people kept away from me by law. We didn't say much for five minutes or so until

Andrew suddenly stopped and grabbed my arm.

"Don't come to my house," he said. "Go away, go back to your town."

I was surprised by his change of mind. "But you agreed to let me sleep in your bed."

Andrew unbuttoned his shirt and exposed an ugly scar running from his left shoulder to his right waist. "We're an angry people and would love to kill a white." He explained that some of the guys we had been talking with were lying in wait for me around the next corner.

My mind exploded with rage at the diabolical separation we were forced to live with as I ran very fast to somewhere I don't remember. Andrew had saved my life for some reason I'll probably never know, and he no doubt suffered the consequences at the hands of his peers.

It's humbling to be protected by the one you oppress. Later I wished I hadn't run from Andrew, but had to live with what may have been the folly of my heart that took me to that disenfranchised town in the first place.

7
"A Brutal Jesus"

God and country: the two are inseparable.

The preamble to the South African constitution sets the mood for all legislative and judicial actions: "In humble submission to Almighty God, who controls the destinies of nations and the history of peoples; who gathered our forebears together from many lands and gave them this their own. . . . "

It was God who put the Dutch farmers on South African soil; it was God who determined it should be ruled in accordance with the scheme that the rest of the constitution outlines. So what can the Afrikaners do as good Christians except humbly submit to His divine will?

The opening sentence of the "Programme and Principles" of the ruling Nationalist Party states: "The Party acknowledges the sovereignty and guidance of God in the destinies of nations and people, and seeks the development of our national life along Christian National lines."

This God-language did not accidentally slip into these official documents. Ever since the Battle of Blood River, it's been God and Afrikaner, hand in hand, creating and governing the Republic of South Africa.

Perhaps one of the greatest tragedies in the history of the country is the role one of its most prominent religious leaders played in securing the system of apartheid. Andrew Murray was one of the Western world's leading revivalists. Born in South Africa, Murray not only wrote prolifically about holiness, humility and the worldwide demands of the gospel, he preached tirelessly throughout the nation and founded a missions training school that thrust dozens of white Afrikaners into black and colored areas to teach about the love of Jesus.

Sadly, at a critical juncture in apartheid's development, Murray encouraged a proposal that separated races in their worship. As blacks and coloreds became Christians, they were drawn to white churches. Suddenly white Christians were confronted with their own slaves and servants worshiping in church with them, and even sharing the same communion cup. Whites weren't willing to drink from a cup used by a black in their homes; they weren't willing to do it in church, either.

If anything ought to unite Christians, one would expect it to be the act of remembering how Jesus gave up everything to the point of humiliation, suffering and death so that we, not because of our greatness but rather precisely because of our need, could become redeemed and accepted as His brothers and sisters.

Instead, this act of communion became the dividing line, clearly marking the limits of white submission to the gospel's demand that Jesus' followers live as He did. Even more than that, it uncovered their perspective that somehow they were superior creatures, unquestionably more noble than the blacks, and apparently above the groveling behavior of their own Saviour.

So, in 1857, Rev. Andrew Murray, in deference to the

"weakness of his brothers" in the Dutch Reformed Church mandated separate communion, separate church buildings, a separate gospel. It's a sobering experience to stand at his grave in the courtyard of the church he pastored for several years, just across the street from his missions training school, and to realize how fragile a human being really is; to understand with hindsight the full impact of a drastic decision made by one of God's leaders who should have fought for the fullness of the gospel rather than acquiescing to the self-centeredness of his subjects.

The Dutch Reformed Church continued steadily in this tradition. When the British still controlled the South African legislature, the top leaders of the Dutch Reformed Church constantly petitioned for legalized separation in all other aspects of the nation's life. They requested their prime ministers to legislate separate living areas, separate schools, separate universities and to outlaw marriage between the races. Regularly turned down by the colonial leaders, the Afrikaner Church finally tasted victory in 1948 when its Nationalist Party took control of the parliament.

They won by a narrow margin at the booths, but less than a decade later, they enjoyed 80 percent of the popular white vote. The English-speaking population, which earlier had refused to endorse apartheid measures, quickly became supportive of the system. They didn't sense the religious mandate of the Dutch Reformed Church, but the new system benefited all whites, and English church leaders found the convenience too enticing. They echoed Afrikaner rationales for this separation and today have, for all practical purposes, become fully Afrikanerized.

Dr. David Bosch is both a "liberated" Afrikaner and one of South Africa's leading theologians. He sees the Dutch Reformed Church as a civil religion which "functions as a supportive organism within the political set-up. Here the church does not just silently endure whatever the state is doing; she actually applauds and endorses the state's policies."

The consequences, of course, are devastating for the Church. Says Bosch, "The Church gradually ceases to be critical to the state's programs and actions; she provides supernatural sanction to the government's policies; almost imperceptibly she changes from being a *religious* community to being an *ideological* community. She receives more and more privileges from the state, but ultimately at the expense of her own soul. She gradually tends to obey the state rather than God."

The most tragic consequence of this link between the church and apartheid is the fact that it defames the name of Christ before blacks in South Africa, and before the world's nations that look on. Apartheid challenges the very integrity of the church and the credibility of the Christian faith.

When President Botha describes his policies as reflections of "Christian principles," the world sees modeled a brutal Jesus who is a tyrannical despot of the worst sort, destroying blacks for the benefit of whites. The list of crimes committed against blacks by apartheid is almost endless: Families are ripped apart; millions are forcibly removed to uninhabitable, death-producing regions. Those who protest are tortured with electric shocks to the genitals; they are suspended upside down, beaten, starved and raped. To the watching world that sees these crimes and hears the white "God talk," it looks like all of it is being done in the name of Jesus.

The evil of apartheid supplies fuel to many anti-Christian movements that claim to have more sympathy for human suffering than these followers of Jesus. A pamphlet widely distributed in Africa states: "In the Republic of South Africa, the Christian religion has . . . done the most harm." The tract encourages its readers to consider Islam, which offers "freedom from slavery and exploitation, social economic and political justice between man and man, equality, dignity and brotherhood among mankind."

Marxists are also having a heyday over apartheid. When Marx called religion the "opiate of the people," could he have imagined how religion would be used to keep 22 million blacks in submission to whites, with only heaven to look forward to? Marxist movements around the world regularly refer to South Africa as the contemporary justification of their ideology, the most dramatic proof of how Christianity, capitalism and the rest of Western culture always result in the oppression of masses of people.

While Christians around the world express their support for "that Christian, democratic country," Muslims, Marxists and people of every political persuasion in the third world denounce South Africa as "that racist Christian country." They see Jesus as the author of racism, not the One who died to break down the dividing wall between peoples.

"Don't you find yourself recoiling in shame?" I ask Christians sometimes. "Don't you find yourself jealous for the name of Christ, embarrassed at the misrepresentation of the gospel? Aren't you crushed by the millions in Africa who have turned to Islam because they see in it a religion that treats blacks better than does Christianity?"

As a white South African, I've had to seriously question the legitimacy of Christianity. I went through a personal crisis of faith where I was confronted with a biblical view of Christianity that seemed absolutely opposed to the life-style of the South African Church. Repeated searching in the Scriptures continually brought me back to the most basic commands Christ gave His Church: "Love the Lord your God with all your heart and with all your soul and with all your mind," and "Love your neighbor as yourself."[1]

"Love does no harm to its neighbor," states Roman 13.[2] Apartheid stands in direct contradiction to the love command.

White South Africa has the highest percentage of churchgoers of any nation in the world. And yet, every Sunday the whites unite in prayer, hymns, Holy Communion and Bible teaching without so much as a whisper of repentance for how they treat blacks.

I've had to ask myself, "What makes someone a Christian?" I acknowledge that inside me lives a beast. It's capable of the most hideous of crimes against my fellow human beings, but it has been chained—not because of my heroic dragon-slaying attempts, but simply because at one point in my life I became a follower of Christ. I received forgiveness for my sins and eternal life, but that's not all. Within me was released a gentle Spirit that finds His origin in God. It looks mercifully at the downtrodden and begins to love them as though they were my very own brothers and sisters. That same Holy Spirit moves me to follow the example of Christ who does not live for Himself, but rather gave up all to live for the best interests of others.

It is precisely that locking up of the beast and the creation of a completely new person inside me through the work of the Holy Spirit that makes me a Christian. Once I was controlled by the evil one; now I'm controlled by the Servant King.

Does white South Africa know this same Servant King? Has it been recreated by the same Holy Spirit? At times I want to shout out a resolute no! Inside the Church lives a wild, unchained beast that is wreaking havoc and controlling the minds of its white subjects who bear the name of Christ!

It's not mine to judge, however. Only God Himself has the privilege and the responsibility of determining who it is that truly belongs to Him. But the Scriptures are abundantly clear that those who love God *do* love their neighbors. The white South African Church will have to face God's judgment of its deeds.

The Nationalist Party publishes a monthly party organ, *The Nationalist.* Each issue appropriately has a little section entitled "Meditation." A sketch of an open Bible with two hands reverently resting on its pages sets the tone for a party, a people, a government living out the message of the Scriptures.

The February 1986, meditation calls the reader to Mark 7:21-23: "From within, out of men's hearts, come evil thoughts, sexual immorality, theft, murder, adultery, greed, malice, deceit, lewdness, envy, slander, arrogance and folly. All these evils come from inside and make a man 'unclean.'"

It escapes me how a Christian government official in South Africa is able to read this passage for inspiration as he goes about enforcing apartheid, which without question actively promotes theft, murder, greed, malice, deceit and arrogance.

I read the whole chapter of Mark 7 after reading this little inspiration and couldn't help but wonder if verse 6 was recorded partly for the white Church of South Africa: "These people honor me with their lips, but their hearts are far from me."

Yes, the world has seen a brutal Jesus, but that's not

the same Jesus the book of Mark shows us, the Jesus who told us to drink the communion cup together in memory of His love.

Notes
1. Matthew 22:37,39.
2. Romans 13:10.

8
No Connections

Every Saturday evening the Dominee (Afrikaner preacher) across the street backed his Mercedes Benz out of his double-car garage. It became a weekly ritual for me to watch him and wonder about his seeming innocence as he went about this religious duty.

Before long a couple of dozen blacks would be arriving from surrounding white homes where they worked as house servants. They lived in "servant's quarters"—the tiny one-room additions behind every garage in the neighborhood. Government building codes required they be put there, with only a toilet (no sink or shower) provided.

It was always a curious point to me that the same builders who built lovely homes for whites never managed to build these servant quarters with the same warmth as the rest of the house. It was even more curious to me that of all the homes I ever stayed in, those built by missionaries had the worst servant's quarters—the only toilet supplied for their laborers was a flush hole in the ground. Inside the main house, the missionaries enjoyed the modern versions.

I would watch from my window as these black servants filtered in through one of the garage doors and sat on old wooden crates or the floor. Before long, they harmonized in beautiful singing in a way that only blacks seem capable of. A little later, the Dominee offered a sermon and a prayer, and off they went again to their quarters.

A black church meeting in a double-car garage shouldn't mean anything, except that on the other side of the Dominee's manse was an expansive, modern church, fully equipped with pipe organ, padded pews especially designed for the comfort of pregnant women and well-designed acoustics to ensure a lovely delivery of God's Word. Sunday morning that building would come alive as an all-white congregation—many of them employers of the servants who worshiped in the garage the night before—happily made its way into the sanctuary. Daylight and fancy, colorful clothing made for quite a contrast to those blacks who were always dressed down and arrived in the dark after a good day's work.

I used to wonder if this contrast ever made an impression on the Dominee. I'd listen to his sermons, and there was no doubt that he would warm up any pew-sitter with his hell-fire preaching. Yet somehow his teaching never filtered down to the realities of apartheid. His church members in this little town of Monte Vista would never be forced to think that Christianity went much beyond baptism, regular attendance and two collections per service.

Our family often invited this Dominee to our house. Sipping tea in our living room, he exhibited all the gentle characteristics of a Christian, one whom I would easily call "brother." I could never muster the wherewithal as a 13-year-old to inquire if the Dominee felt the same awkwardness I did as I watched the little black congregation in his garage on Saturday nights. I also never asked him what he thought of Monte Vista's "parent patrol."

Monte Vista was a government project of sorts for white integration. Half of the residents were South African citizens, the other half were made up of Dutch, Germans, Britons, Scots, Australians, Americans and Portuguese. All these different little white tribes, the government hoped, would live together peacefully and, thus, continue to demonstrate white superiority.

As a fairly new town, Monte Vista was bordered by bush on three sides. Police vans appeared every so often, but residents didn't feel adequately protected from blacks roaming the bush. A police-sanctioned "parent-patrol" was created, and fathers combed the bush and walked the streets in groups of three or more during the evenings. These vigilantes experienced the power of enforcing law and order. Like the regular police, they also had a certain latitude in deciding the criminal's fate. One evening as the vigilantes were preparing to go out together, some of us teenagers overheard them swapping stories about their search efforts in the bush.

Any black who was caught was automatically a criminal. Justice could be measured out in any number of ways—beating the captive, stripping him naked and then chasing him through the bush for a while like a frightened animal unsure of its end or taking him to the police station. Women caught in the bush, however, presented another whole range of possibilities. The men laughed as they described what it was like to watch a woman have to choose between rape or the police station—where she would be fined and possibly raped anyway.

Rape. What system could create such beasts who would treat mothers and daughters this way? The majority of white South Africans do not go around finding victims, torturing them and then boasting of their sport. But it does happen regularly, not only in the bush, but also in the prisons.

Without a doubt, the Dominee, a "high-cultured" white South African, would find the rape story an offensive intrusion into our British-style afternoon tea. And yet I was sure that he, like other sincere adults I discussed this with, would never imagine that the enjoyment of his life-style brought affliction upon the blacks making his tea.

Why would he recoil in horror at the rape story, but not at the daily plight of the black servants in Monte Vista? The diabolical consequence of apartheid is that, every day and all day long, millions of blacks are violated. They suffer from fear, starvation, abuse, sickness and separation from the ones they love. And yet very few whites seem to be repulsed.

No connections.

Somehow the elders of Monte Vista Dutch Reformed Church missed the connection between what the Church meant to them and the despicable condition the black laborers who built the church lived in at Langa, unceremoniously shoved into crowded cattle-style conditions.

Somehow the white mother whose life went so much easier because of her live-in servant missed the connection between her cozy living room Bible studies and the heartaches of the woman doing the ironing in the kitchen, who had to live separated from her husband in order to find work.

Somehow every Sunday the white Christians of South Africa can take Holy Communion without blushing at the instructions that accompany the sacrament: "Whoever eats the bread or drinks the cup of the Lord in an unworthy manner will be guilty of sinning against the body and blood of the Lord. A man ought to examine himself before he eats of the bread and drinks of the cup. For anyone who eats and drinks without recognizing the body of the Lord [the Christian family] eats and drinks judgment on himself."[1]

No connections.

Reflecting on this dilemma, David Bosch told me, "Our most serious guilt, to which we must confess, is the sin of which we are not aware."

Perhaps some are not aware. But few can legitimately ignore the escalating violence in the townships, and the mounting pressures from other countries that indicate something is sorely amiss. Few can say with a clear conscience that they do no harm to their neighbor, and continue to live in the luxury of a white South Africa supported by black slave labor.

At least, not if the love of Jesus Christ has exploded in their hearts.

> Now listen, you rich people, weep and wail because of the misery that is coming upon you. Your wealth has rotted, and moths have eaten your clothes. Your gold and silver are corroded. Their corrosion will testify against you and eat your flesh like fire. You have hoarded wealth in the last days. Look! The wages you failed to pay the workmen who mowed your fields are crying out against you. The cries of the harvesters have reached the ears of the Lord Almighty. You have lived on earth in luxury and self-indulgence. You have fattened yourselves in the day of slaughter. You have condemned

and murdered innocent men, who were not opposing you.[2]

> You trample on the poor and force him to give you grain. Therefore, though you have built stone mansions, you will not live in them;
> though you have planted lush vineyards, you will not drink their wine.
> For I know how many are your offenses and how great your sins.
> You oppress the righteous and take bribes and you deprive the poor of justice in the courts . . . .
> Seek good, not evil, that you may live.
> Then the Lord God Almighty will be with you, just as you say he is.
> Hate evil, love good; maintain justice in the courts . . . .
> I hate, I despise your religious feasts; I cannot stand your assemblies.
> Even though you bring me burnt offerings and grain offerings, I will not accept them.
> Though you bring choice fellowship offerings, I will have no regard for them.
> Away with the noise of your songs!
> I will not listen to the music of your harps,
> But let justice roll on like a river.[3]

Notes
1. 1 Corinthians 11:27-29.
2. James 5:1-6.
3. Amos 5:11-15; 21-24.

9
Heavenly Minded

"You are a man of God. You cannot go into politics. You have no idea how dirty it can be."

Those were the stern words of the wife of Prime Minister Vorster to David du Plessis, the pastor of their church. Someone had suggested Du Plessis might make a successful candidate; his parishioners were quick to disagree.

Known around the world as "Mr. Pentecostal," Du Plessis was born and raised in South Africa, and has lived in the United States for the past 40 years. Although both he and his wife are pushing toward their 90s, they remain active in their globe-trotting attempts to bring unity to the Church worldwide.

When Mrs. Vorster warned him of the dangers of politics, Du Plessis was the General Secretary of the Apostolic Faith Mission, a Pentecostal movement born in a little black church in 1908. Of his leadership in this movement Du Plessis told me, "I exercised apartheid in the Church long before it became a political term." Preachers and pastors of the various tribes used to minister to people of all the other tribes, Du Plessis explained, rather than only those who spoke the same language. Du Plessis made a rule: "Zulu to Zulu, Xhosa to Xhosa, Sotho to Sotho."

Mrs. Vorster's words to Du Plessis aptly illustrate the irony of many South African Christians who think church leaders should stay out of politics. What escaped her was that Du Plessis was *already* a political person. He was one of the great sculptors of apartheid within his own religious circles. Even today, though he thinks of himself primarily as a "minister of the gospel," he continues to defend the political structure of apartheid. "It's not the South Africans that are the sinners," he says, "it's all the nations that interfere where they've got no business to." Through his role in Pentecostal churches in South Africa and worldwide, he influences the political thinking of many Christians, perhaps more than politicians do.

The Church in South Africa is heavenly minded. Christians think they are called to operate only in the spiritual realm and fail to see their influence on the political realm. They never claim to be apolitical: They vote, usually along Nationalistic lines. They have worked hard to see legislation passed that shuts down most of the nation's stores on Sunday because that's the "Lord's day." They've also lobbied for tight liquor and gambling controls. But when it comes to the government "system" of apartheid, which regulates human rights and racial discrimination, they "stay out of politics."

Even those who oppose apartheid find themselves paralyzed when it comes to the political realm. Their heavenly minded Christianity doesn't tell them how to work to see justice established.

Ralph Christensen, veteran missionary to South Africa

for 35 years, recognizes the inadequacies of this orientation: "The whole direction of the gospel has been up to heaven rather than incarnational to the world, and therefore, the people don't have a sense of social responsibility. The holistic sense of the gospel has not been taught."

Not enough emphasis has been placed on *discipleship*, asserts Christensen. People have been given the impression that it's possible to become a Christian without going through character changes. "In Christ there is neither Greek nor Jew, black nor white, [but that] has not been taught here." However, Christensen believes that the Church is finally "discovering its call"; in fact, it may be "rediscovering the gospel."

But even as he reflects on the social demands of the gospel, Christensen cannot bring himself to say there are certain elements of the political system of apartheid that must be abolished. He could only offer solutions in the spiritual realm: The Church needs to become the "real Church"; as people's hearts change, so will their society. When I asked him his opinion of black Christian leaders who were demanding one-man-one-vote, he responded, "They shouldn't try to usher in a new political structure unless it reflects Kingdom values." But he can't articulate what changes should occur in the present system to move closer to a reflection of the King.

This doesn't mean he's inactive. Christensen is part of a group that meets regularly with political leaders, praying with and for them, expecting God to work somehow, as together they take a closer look at Christ. "Maybe our ingenuity and our decisions won't bring change—God's going to do it."

Certainly positive change in South Africa is going to come from God. God *always* "does it," but for the most part He accomplishes His work through His people. The evangelical Church in the United States suffered the same kind of political anemia for years, until it finally rallied around the issue of abortion and began to press for legislation that would outlaw the killing of 1.5 million babies in the womb each year. The Church in South Africa, that part that *does* believe in the evil of apartheid, needs to realize that it's time to put aside fuzzy thinking and take action. Their very silence is action: It leaves the government free to continue enforcing legislation that annually kills approximately 100,000 black children before they reach their first birthday.

This heavenly minded Christianity keeps the Church from standing up to apartheid by fostering a spiritual pride. Both the Afrikaner and English-speaking white churches find it easy to brush aside the appeals of other church bodies who are leading the battle against apartheid on the grounds that they've succumbed to "liberal" theology.

The World Alliance of Reformed Churches has suspended the membership of the Dutch Reformed Church until it renounces apartheid. (The historical precedent for this was the suspension of the German Lutheran Church from the World Council of Churches during Hitler's reign because it was unwilling to corporately denounce Hitler's anti-Semitism.) In response to the suspension, the Dutch Reformed Church simply brought out the liberal label. Says Du Plessis, "The Dutch Reformed Church is more Christian than any other reformed church in the world." There's no need to take the suspension seriously because what else would one expect from "pagans" who are trying to tell the Afrikaner Christians how to be more biblical?

To be labeled an ally of the World Council of Churches (WCC) in South African evangelical circles is to be categorized unchristian and never taken seriously. This conven- ient label keeps the whites from ever seriously talking with black Christian leaders for one simple reason: Most of the black churches belong to the South African Council of Churches (SACC), which is connected to the WCC. The whites can't see that the SACC churches are attempting to make the Bible their standard for Christian practice and to understand the call to "love your neighbor as yourself" in its very specific application in the South African context. They simply write their black brothers and sisters off as not being "real Christians."

Leaders of several black denominations met with other members of the WCC last year in Zimbabwe to discuss the "emergency" dimensions of South Africa's crisis. The Gospel Defense League newsletter carried a photograph of the South African delegation with Dr. Emilio Castro, General Secretary of the WCC. That was all they had to say to dismiss the conference and those who attended it.

The same newsletter closed with the evangelicals' solution to South Africa's crisis: "Imagine what South Africa would be like if every man, woman and child was a *Christian,* if they would all think, talk, live and act like Christians!"

That's exactly what the SACC is pleading for. They want the love and the power of heaven to be a reality in the lives of Christians, not just something in their minds.

10
Paying the Bills

White South Africa has lived well. Yet they can't legitimately claim that their good life is simply the result of their hard, honest labor and the blessing of Western technology. The luxury they enjoy today is inseparable from the cheap labor they control.

South African whites are going to face some serious changes if they decide to adjust to the biblical requirement of treating others justly. In a sense, it's time to pay the bills. Their comfort has been financed by their servants, and if they move forward justly, they are going to have to become servants, in the strictest biblical sense, of the blacks.

The Church has proclaimed a cheap Christianity. It has lived for more than a hundred years now as though the only real Christian duty is to wait around on earth, doing business-as-usual, until God takes it home for the heavenly reward of eternal life. Racial unrest and foreign press is causing the Church to question the legitimacy of that stand.

Those who are going back to their Bibles are finding there's a price to pay: Just as Jesus was crucified for the sake of our reconciliation to Him, so there is no escape from the cross for people who claim to follow that same Christ. There is no middle ground. The crucifixion that the Church will need to go through is reconciliation— accepting the suffering that is going to be a part of making right the wrongs it has done to black brothers and sisters.

Deitrich Bonhoeffer, a German theologian who was executed by Hitler for his revolutionary role against the Nazi state, has gone down in history as a man who reestablished the standard for following Christ. In his book *The Cost of Discipleship,* Bonhoeffer states: "When Christ bids a man come, he bids him come and die."[1]

I believe 50 years from now, the Christian world will acknowledge Dr. David Bosch as the Bonhoeffer of South Africa, a man way ahead of his time. An Afrikaner by heritage, Bosch has led the theological battle against apartheid for several decades now.

Perhaps the clearest call that has yet come from within the Church for reconciliation and justice in South Africa is Bosch's address at the National Initiative for Reconciliation in September 1985. This event brought together church leaders from all races and denominations to seek biblical solutions to apartheid. Bosch's keynote address focused on the need to move away from "cheap reconciliation" and to follow the costly path of reconciliation through the cross.

Bosch labeled "cheap reconciliation" the "deadly enemy of the Church." Those who think that everyone becoming Christians or being born again will automatically solve South Africa's problems are proponents of this cheap grace. "Cheap reconciliation means tearing faith and justice asunder," said Bosch. It "means driving a wedge between the vertical and horizontal. It suggests we can have peace with God without having justice in our mutual relationships." It's like treating cancer with aspirin; South Africa's injustices require radical surgery.

Bosch challenged the Church to accept the radical costs of true reconciliation. Reconciliation strikes the deepest elements of our lives and requires us to give up the very things we think we can't live without.

"The gospel challenges us to be willing to give up our privileges . . . to leave self behind," said Bosch. Once apartheid is identified as sin, the gospel calls for a response. "It urges us to stop all this and put it right, now, regardless of the consequences. And I say that because I mean it: regardless of the consequences.

"We know that, at least as we perceive it, this involves tremendous risks. But the gospel challenges us to do justice now—even if the world comes to an end, our world. We know that only if we accept this and get up and do it, shall we really be free to obey. Only if this is the road we walk, only if we truly leave self behind, shall we be free to live in a country in which we no longer have any say. Live in it and serve in it while we truly experience and enjoy the freedom of the Kingdom of the children of God."

Bosch pulled no punches, but dealt with what to white South Africans is the unthinkable: They must do justly "even if a future South Africa turns out to be one ruled by a corrupt and oppressive Marxist regime, and we have to give up all those things to which we have clung always for dear life. I don't say this out of defeatism. Neither am I suggesting that I would welcome a Marxist regime. I believe that the communist system is something abhorrent. And I can't claim that I'm not afraid.

"We should begin thinking about the possible emergence of a situation in which we may become the underdogs. I'm submitting that we should be able to continue being Christians even in such circumstances. The Church of Christ is alive and surviving today, even in Russia and China and Vietnam and Iran. I suggest that the Church in the catacombs is the Church in a truer sense of the word than the Church in the palaces. It is, for one thing, liberated from the guilt of privilege and from its bad conscience.

"I am aware that this may involve martyrdom, but martyrdom has always been one of the disciplines that the Church has survived. After all, the blood of the martyrs is the seed of the Church. I am saying this with fear and trembling. I know myself and my own weaknesses too well to make in confidence this kind of statement about willingness to be a servant in a context where I may be the underdog and the oppressed. But again, that's not my concern now. Not what others might do, but what I should do is my concern now. And therefore, I can only say I will do it. May God have mercy on me."[2]

Ultimately, the Church must follow Jesus' example, especially as that example leads to the cross. This is the "normal Christian life," said Bosch, for it was Jesus' scars that were the proof of His identity to His disciples. Jesus demonstrated a painful reconciliation not only in His death on the cross, but in His entire ministry:

> He is the Good Samaritan who risks His life for a Jew, who is really supposed to be His archenemy. He is the Good Shepherd who puts His life in jeopardy for every obstinate sheep. He is the servant who washes the feet even of His betrayer. He is the master who loves the rich young ruler while knowing that the young man

would not be prepared to pay the price of discipleship. He is the One who reinstates Peter in his office, even if Peter had denied Him in His hour of trial. He is the master who trusts His disciples sufficiently to send them to the ends of the earth, even while knowing that they have all deserted Him and fled in the hour of trial. Supremely, He is the One who prays for those who crucified Him, "Father, forgive them, for they do not know what they are doing."[3]

Bosch continued: "It is of such a man that we are called to be disciples, and it is totally out of the question that we shall be His disciples without getting hurt ourselves. Moreover, unless I get hurt, I can't help others who hurt. It is only through wounds that wounds can be healed. Isn't that what the prophet said? 'He was pierced for our transgressions, he was crushed for our iniquities. The punishment that brought us peace was upon him. By his wounds we are healed.'[3]

"The scorners mocked Him. 'He saved others, . . . he can't save himself!'[5] But this is just the point. This Christ who saved others but did not save Himself, reveals in that the fundamental character of the true God. False gods save themselves. They don't save others. By implication this is true of false Christians also. They save themselves, not others.

"True Christians are to ever, says Paul, bear on their bodies the scars of Jesus inflicted by other people. They carry around in their mortal bodies the death of Jesus. They are like people condemned to death in the arena. A spectacle to the whole universe. Fools for Christ's sake. Where the world shouts hatred, they say love. Where the world demands violence, they bring peace. Where the world cries for vengeance, they offer forgiveness. They thus turn everything upside down almost as if nothing makes sense any longer. It is the dying who still live on and the sorrowful who have cause for joy. It is the poor who bring wealth to many and the penniless who own the world. This is the paradox of the Christian life. It is when we are weak we are strong."[6]

The father of the boy with an evil spirit could only say "Lord, I do believe. Help me overcome my unbelief."[7] Lord, I am willing. Help me overcome my unwillingness.

"We are, after all," said Bosch, "not only talking about the processes of reconciliation, but also about demands of obedience. Of course, I would have preferred the change in our country to come because of the promptings of the Spirit of God and not because of the terrible events we are experiencing these days. Biblically, I would have preferred change to come because of the repentance of Israel; not because of the batterings of Assyria. But this is often the way God works. If our hearts are hardened to His Spirit, He uses other means. And the executors of His judgment may surprise us.

"It is not sufficient to have national days of prayer and repentance and fasting, unless we also do restitution."

Bosch points to the instruction of Isaiah 58:

> Shout it aloud, do not hold back.
>   Raise your voice like a trumpet.
> Declare to my people their rebellion and to the
>   house of Jacob their sins.
> For day after day they seek me out; they seem
>   eager to know my ways,
> as if they were a nation that does what is right

and has not forsaken the commands of its
    God.
They ask me for just decisions and seem eager
    for God to come near them.
"Why have we fasted," they say,
    "and you have not seen it?
Why have we humbled ourselves,
    and you have not noticed?"
Yet on the day of your fasting, you do as you
    please and exploit all your workers . . . .
You cannot fast as you do today and expect your
    voice to be heard on high.
Is this the kind of fast I have chosen,
    only a day for a man to humble himself?
Is it only for bowing one's head like a reed and
    for lying on sackcloth and ashes?
Is that what you call a fast,
    a day acceptable to the Lord?
Is not this the kind of fasting I have chosen:
        to loose the chains of injustice and untie the
        cords of the yoke,
        to set the oppressed free and break every
        yoke?[8]

"If that happens," said Bosch, "we will be freer than
we've ever been before. We will stand empty-handed but
free, under God's open heaven."

Bosch warned that reconciliation is not an option, but a
demand of the gospel. "God forgives our debts as we forgive our debtors.[9] He does not forgive us *if* we forgive our
debtors, but there is a link there, nevertheless. We cannot
receive God's forgiveness and remain unyielding to our
human debtors."

To refuse to be reconciled, Bosch went on, is to crucify Christ anew. "We are saying, in effect, that what
Christ did is of no consequence. The middle wall of parti-
tion is as solid as ever. It is as though Christ had never
come. Not to believe in the possibility of reconciliation and
not to act as people who have found and embraced one
another, who really love one another with an indestructible
love, who serve one another, who act justly toward one
another, not to do all this actually means reinforcing and
buttressing that wall that divides us. The question, 'Are
you prepared to be reconciled to your brother and sister?'
is in essence the same as the question, 'Do you believe in
the Lord Jesus Christ?' We cannot divorce the two.

"The bridge [to reconciliation] is already there. Our
Lord in His own body of flesh and blood has broken down
the enmity which stood like a dividing wall between us. He
is the bridge over which we cross to each other again and
again."

Bosch has not only provided invaluable insights to the
biblical path reconciliation will require, but he's been honest and personal about his own weakness and turmoil as
he looks into the face of those demands. No doubt the tes-
timony of his life will lead others to similar steps of reconciliation.

Bishop Tutu is supplying a parallel model of reconciliation for the black community. He's honest about the internal struggle: "Sometimes I want to hate my enemy. When
my child picks up the phone and gets a call intended for her
daddy, and she stands there trembling because of the
ghastly things she's hearing on the telephone, I really want
to hate."

But Tutu believes that Scripture demands a higher
way: "I'm supposed to bless those who curse me."[10]

Tutu says that the black soul is hurting. People hurt because their mothers and daughters are being raped by soldiers, the very people the white community regards as friends and protectors. They hurt because they've been "raped of citizenship," because when they drive home at night, they can't drive into their community before the police strip and search their wives and daughters. They hurt because they experience all the human emotions that whites experience. They hurt because their dignity is rubbed in the dirt and trampled underfoot.

Tutu asks his white brothers and sisters, "Have you experienced house-to-house searches? Have you been awakened while asleep with your wife by torches shining in your eyes? Have you been emasculated and humiliated by mere whippersnappers (20-year-old policemen) in front of your children?

"You end up wondering whether God cares about black people at all," says Tutu. "And that is the ultimate blasphemy of this ghastly system called apartheid: It makes a child of God doubt that he or she is a child of God."

It is difficult, Tutu intimates, to forgive a person who says, "Forgive me for putting my foot on your neck," while his foot is still on your neck. The Bible instructs us to be reconciled to our *brother*. Brothers must be able to stand upright and look at the other face to face. Tutu quotes the common saying that the missionaries who came to South Africa "stole our land from us while our eyes were closed to say their salvation prayer," but still he's thankful to God for them, because the truth of God Almighty now resides in him and affirms his dignity and worth. Says he, "We are taking our Bible seriously."

The ability to forgive in the face of persecution comes to Tutu because of the work of the Holy Spirit in his life.

"The spiritual is absolutely central—our resources are ultimately spiritual."

Reconciliation is a serious matter. The question is, will the Church be willing to pay the price for this sort of Christianity? A government that claims to be Christian and that receives its lifeblood from the Church will have to decide if it can implement the structures of justice that God demands of governments that bear His name. Or else it will have to drop its "Christian" facade and be frank about its intentions to rule a society in a manner that benefits only the whites.

Either way, Christians who are becoming sensitized by the Spirit of God will be facing a new dilemma as they go to the communion table on Sundays. There they'll have to wrestle with God over their own crucifixion, the crucifixion of their white nationhood and privilege. The journey of discipleship that begins at that point won't be easy, but it will make them free, free to serve God and free to serve black brothers and sisters who have already carried that same cross for three centuries.

Notes
1. Dietrich Bonhoeffer, *The Cost of Discipleship* (Peter Smith, 1983).
2. Subsequent quotes by Bosch are taken from his address at the National Initiative for Reconciliation.
3. Luke 23:34.
4. Isaiah 53:5.
5. Matthew 27:42.
6. See Hebrews 11:33-40.
7. See Mark 9:24.
8. Isaiah 58:1-6.
9. See Matthew 6:12.
10. See Luke 6:28.

11
Cosmetic Changes

When *New York Times* correspondent Joe Lelyveld returned to South Africa in 1980 after several years' absence, one optimistic South African asked him what he thought of the changes that had been made while he was away. Lelyveld responded, "I would never have imagined so much could have been done to improve apartheid."

The government touts the legal changes in the structure of apartheid as great steps forward. They claim that apartheid is an ideal of the past, one that the country is moving away from rapidly. They point the repeal of such cornerstones of apartheid as the Mixed Marriage Act, and more recently, the pass laws. Critics of the system claim that the changes are insubstantial; they merely make apartheid more palatable for "bleeding heart" liberals. Apartheid is a poison that the government now serves to blacks in a silver chalice rather than a tin cup: Certain externals have changed, such as the amount of money the government spends on black education or the number of new box houses it erects for imported labor, but the internal reality remains the same.

Repealing the Mixed Marriage Act and the Immorality

Act no doubt appeared to mark a significant shift in apartheid because they represented a fundamental Afrikaner belief: the need for each race to maintain its separate identity. Afrikaners had fought for years for these acts to become law.

But for the black very little has changed. Lovers of different races won't get arrested anymore for kissing or having sexual intercourse, but that's about the extent of the relief. A black can now marry a white, but they still can't legally live in the same house, ride on the same bus or train, go to the same school or church. They can meet at specially designated "international" hotels meant to accommodate international businessmen and other important people who happened not to have white skin. Most likely, a mixed couple would leave the country and live where a normal relationship could be pursued.

There have been some token changes in the public segregation laws. Certain restaurants have also been designated "international" and can serve blacks. A white may ride on a black train, but not vice versa. Movie theaters are open to all, though very few blacks are able to afford them. The dining cars on cross-country trains have allowed mixed dining since 1984, and a few of the country's beaches have been declared open to all colors, although several now require admission fees. The number of blacks who are in a financial position to take advantage of these new freedoms is so small as to be insignificant. Nothing has changed for the vast majority. Even the most radical step forward—the abolition in April 1986, of the passbook blacks had been required to carry at all times—turned out to be a sham in that the passbook was simply replaced with a more sophisticated "life-book" that all races must carry.

What the government champions as significant steps forward in abolishing the system of apartheid have been nothing more than cosmetic. A black may be on the national dart-throwing team, but he still goes home to crowded Soweto, still is grossly underpaid, still has no privilege whatsoever to determine the political future of his nation, still hurts with the knowledge that millions of his people continue to die of starvation, disease and hardship.

What the blacks think of these changes can be seen in the increasing unrest in the black community since the new Constitution gave coloreds and Indians a limited participation in government; 1985 was the worst year of unrest and violence in recent memory. According to police statistics more than 1,000 blacks died by police bullets (although some church leaders claim the figure is several thousand). Thousands more blacks were imprisoned for political reasons, including 1,000 children under the age of seven.

The United Democratic Front (UDF) is unquestionably the single largest political opposition group in South Africa. It has spearheaded most of the nonviolent protest of the government's actions, from the boycott of elections to the new colored and Indian Houses of Parliament to peaceful demonstrations at the funerals of those slain by police.

Funerals are one of the few forms of political expression left for blacks in South Africa, and the UDF tries to show its support at as many as possible. Sometimes there are also communist flags and banners at the scene, and the government predictably has claimed that the UDF is a communist organization. Allan Boesak, founder of the UDF responds to that claim: "I resent that [label]; I am a Christian minister. My opposition to apartheid is exactly based upon my Christian beliefs. I do not believe in any form of communism . . . . If there is anybody that is actually furthering the aims of communism and making people believe that communism ought to be looked at as a viable alternative, it is the government."

During 1985, the government arrested all the UDF leadership and accused them of treason. Boesak's high visibility and the close attention of the international community eventually forced the government to drop the charges and release the prisoners.

When blacks in South Africa look for an agenda for political change, they usually look to the African National Congress (ANC), the oldest resistance movement. In 1912, black leaders of every tribe represented in South Africa met to plead with the British government for their inclusion as full citizens of the Union. Their request was denied, and the ANC was born as a non-violent political voice for the country's majority, trying to influence legislation toward equality and multi-racial government.

In 1955, the ANC called a "Congress of the People," bringing together 2,888 delegates. Out of this meeting came the "Freedom Charter," adopted unanimously by the Congress and still the principal statement of the government black South Africans are working to see established.

Nothing about the text of the Charter would be offensive to Christian or democratic values—in fact, quite the opposite. The Charter rings with the same spirit one can imagine filled the room in Philadelphia as the founding fathers signed the American Declaration of Independence. Yet a year after the Charter was signed, 156 of the ANC leaders were arrested for treason; four years after that the ANC was banned completely. The government of South Africa obviously looks at this as a subversive document, though the United Nations has endorsed it as a just standard for a future South Africa, and most Americans would recognize the changes it calls for as basic, "inalienable" rights of the citizens of any civilized country. Here are the preamble and basic tenants of the charter; the full text appears in Appendix 1.

> We, the people of South Africa, declare for all our country and the world to know:
> —that South Africa belongs to all who live in it, black and white, and that no government can justly claim authority unless it is based on the will of all the people;
> —that our people have been robbed of their birthright to land, liberty and peace by a form of government founded on injustice and inequality;
> —that our country will never be prosperous or free until all our people live in brotherhood, enjoying equal rights and opportunities;
> —that only a democratic state, based on the will of all the people, can secure to all their birthright without distinction of colour, race, sex or belief;
> And therefore, we the people of South Africa, black and white together—equals, countrymen and brothers—adopt this Freedom Charter. And we pledge ourselves to strive together, sparing neither strength nor courage, until the democratic changes set out here have been won.

The document goes on to call for true democracy including all of South Africa's people, where all have the right to vote and participate in government. It calls for equal rights and equal standing of all before the law. The Charter mandates equal economic opportunity in access to mineral wealth, land and jobs. It calls for equality in education and culture, and in social services such as housing and medical care. Finally, it calls on South Africa to live at peace with its neighbors and recognize their rights to be free and self-governing.

Most black South Africans would still endorse the Freedom Charter today. But one of the most significant changes in black opposition strategy since the Charter was signed occurred in 1960. In a township called Sharpeville, a crowd of blacks had met for a political discussion. Police arrived on the scene to disperse the crowd. Sixty-nine blacks died, all of them shot in the back while fleeing the police. In the outrage following Sharpeville, the ANC decided that violence was their only means to see change in the government policies. The government outlawed the ANC and imprisoned its leader Nelson Mandela, for life.

Tragically, the ANC has continued in its use of violence, and innocent people have been killed by their attacks over the past 25 years. It should be noted, however, that more black civilians were killed on the average *per week* during 1985 by white police, than *all* civilians killed by ANC revolutionaries in its entire 25-year history of commitment to violence.

As with the UDF, the government has labelled the ANC communist. There can be no denying that the ANC has cooperated with communists since the inception of the South African Communist Party in 1921. The ANC finds communism more attractive than apartheid (to the shame of the Christian Church), but flatly denies that it is a communist organization. The ANC is a *nationalistic* movement, the elder statesman of the black human-rights movement in South Africa.

The ANC is also caring for thousands of refugees across the border who have escaped political harassment in South Africa. These camps are known to be operated efficiently and humanely.

The ANC has a vision of a nonracial South Africa, and they invite whites to join their liberation movement. Says Oliver Tambo, current president of the ANC, "What we hope our white compatriots will learn to understand is that we don't really see them as whites in the first instance. We see them as fellow South Africans."

The only outrightly Marxist opposition group is the Azanian People's Organization (AZAPO), named after Azania, as the blacks intend to call the liberated South Africa. AZAPO grew dramatically during 1984, capturing the imagination especially of youth, but with the capable leadership of Boesak at the helm of the UDF, AZAPO has slowly but surely dwindled in the shadow of the ever-increasing UDF.

The vast majority of South Africa's blacks are calling for peaceful change toward a future democratic system of government for South Africa. The whites continue to answer their pleas and their unrest with petty changes and increasing totalitarian control. Fear controls the white population, fear that there will be cataclysmic change should the blacks come to power, fear that there will be no place for them, and most of all fear that change will mean a victory for the communists, the end of life-as-they-know-it in South Africa.

12
Communists in My Backyard

The high school I attended in South Africa had periodic "terrorist drills." Supposedly we faced the threat of a bunch of communists showing up at our school ready to take innocent children hostage and to blow the building apart. Their strategy would be to land on our roof with helicopters.

The school bell rang during terrorist drills, signaling us to leave the building and march to the rugby field (the procedure was identical to our fire drills). The whole thing always seemed silly to me, as I pictured terrorists firing down on us from the roof with submachine guns. I doubt the officials who dreamed up the drill seriously thought we'd ever face the real attack; the pragmatic value of the drills was to keep us ever mindful of South Africa's "real" enemy: communism.

During my latest trip to South Africa, I visited the Supreme Court building in Cape Town. Kobus Joubert, a security officer, stood guard at the doorway. I explained I was a journalist from the United States, and we talked about South Africa for a while.

118 Apartheid: Tragedy in Black and White

Kobus was quick to tell me that he was not allowed to "talk politics," but wanted me to set the record straight for Americans. "I'm a Christian," he said. "I want to tell you the truth, God's truth. All of our problems here are because of the communists. They want to overthrow the government, and they're working through people like Bishop Tutu."

I prodded Kobus about his communist theory. "Are you sure the current unrest doesn't have something to do with the poverty blacks live in because of the apartheid system?"

"The media lies about the situation here," he responded. "I must tell you the truth. The blacks have all the same rights as white; they just seem to prefer to live in smaller homes. I think it's because they're basically tribal."

Kobus is no extreme Afrikaner. Like all other white South Africans, he's been raised with the view that any threat to the current system is communist; any opposition person is ultimately related to Russia. South Africa, being the God-fearing country that it is, must religiously stamp out any signs of that godless beast. Communism has been apartheid's scapegoat for 30 years now. If the government needs to stamp you out, it simply stamps "communist" on your file. If communism were not in existence, the government would have found some other enemy or rationale.

The communist threat is the most important rationale used by South Africa to explain why it won't change apartheid. The white government must maintain strict control to ensure the communists gain no foothold in the country. Any amount of abuse done to blacks can be justified as a necessary procedure to protect the interests of the nation.

Before I was a teenager, Billy Graham came to South Africa for a major crusade. Before agreeing to come, he made it clear that one of his requirements would be that people of all races could attend. The response of government-controlled media and religious publications was immediate: Underneath that clerical garb, Graham is probably a communist.

Communism poses no greater threat to South Africa than Coca-Cola poses to the United States. The South African Communist Party has never had a significant foothold in the nation and has negligible influence in the unrest in the black townships. Black unrest almost entirely stems from nationalistic ambitions and their desire to be treated like human beings rather than dogs.

Whites believe what the government says. They believe in the reality of the communist threat so strongly that Christians will accept the abuse of 22 million blacks as the only alternative to speaking Russian. Indeed, white Christians take leadership in perpetuating the myth. The Gospel Defense League regularly decries liberation movements and leaders like Tutu as people who think romantically about the Soviet Union, and actually work for Soviet ends.

Christians in South Africa feel the need to speak to their brothers and sisters in other countries to correct the "liberal" view given by the press. Sunday School Supplies, a South-African based Christian publishing house, publishes one such newsletter. Its editor Stanley Legg decries South Africa's ill treatment by liberal journalists and the whole international community. In his opinion, they don't want a real change for the better in South Africa, but "really want a left-wing takeover."

It escapes Legg that black grievances and hardships

might have something to do with internal unrest. It is primarily "left-wing agitation exploiting political issues," fostered by people who are trying to take over the black school system in order "to give instruction in Marxism."

One has to "sympathize" with the police, he asserts, because they have to "perform an impossible task" of dealing with terrorists while balancing that with the "gentle art of diplomacy." The policemen, says Legg, are the defenseless ones, having to protect themselves against angry mobs who "threaten" their lives. He doesn't mention that the police do their duty in armored vehicles and carry grenades, machine guns, tear gas and other military equipment. He doesn't mention that in 1985, four policemen lost their lives during these "threatening" encounters, compared to at least 1,000 blacks, half of them women and children. He *does* mention that the police are protecting themselves from youth who hurl verbal insults, throw five-pound rocks and have access to gasoline bombs.

So the Church moves forward in the name of God and the might of the military to ensure that South Africa remains a decent, civilized nation, free of the threat of communism that doesn't even exist.

Leading Christian groups in the United States have been equally duped by this communist rationale. Jerry Falwell went to South Africa in 1985 with a special delegation that had as its goal to "prove that the American press has had a one-dimensional view of that troubled nation." They found, just as they had suspected all along, that "South Africa's real threat is godless communism."

A few months after that trip, Falwell went on a similar "fact-finding" trip to the Philippines and pleaded with Christian America to support Ferdinand Marcos because he was a champion of human rights, defending that country against the communist threat. Falwell was unable to appreciate that the ground swell of opposition that eventually deposed Marcos was rooted in the Filipinos' desire for just government, rather than rooted in another communist-inspired revolution. Similarly, he couldn't appreciate the reality that black South Africa is simply asking for just, humane treatment.

Upon his return to the United States from South Africa, Falwell published a special 16-page report that, among other things, denounces *all black opposition* as Marxist inspired. And concerning the media in the States, we're told that to them "racism has become far more abhorrent than communist terrorism." In other words, Falwell accepts the rationale that is religiously and forcefully propagated by the South African government and Church: Communism is the only alternative to apartheid. In fact, according to Falwell's report, "The American media will, consciously or unconsciously, continue to serve as willing dupes of the Soviet master planners."

Americans add another twist to the communist threat: Because the Soviet Union is the only other major supplier of certain minerals critical to the U.S. aerospace industry and military weaponry (plutonium, uranium, chromium, cobalt), we dare not let South Africa slip to communism. Otherwise, we'll become totally dependent on the USSR for those critical resources.

In the first place, it's not true that the Soviet Union is the only other major supplier of these resources. Neither has it occurred to these religious leaders that if the United States would be a friendly partner in working for a new, just government structure in that nation, it would have a friendly relationship with a new government—with access to valuable resources as well. (Biblically speaking, Christians are called to work for justice in South Africa without regard for access to these resources.)

Christ for the Nations is a large Pentecostal Bible School in Dallas with a tremendous heritage of sending missionaries around the world. It can claim the amazing accomplishment of having planted over 4,000 third world churches through its alumni. Christ for the Nations has also been duped by the anticommunist rationale for keeping apartheid in place. Freda Lindsay, president of the school, sends out a monthly "world prayer letter" to friends and financial supporters of the school.

Her October 1985, letter has a subheading: "The Destruction of South Africa: U.S. Goal?" In it she concludes that the U.S. media really wants the downfall of South Africa and that surely the result will be a communist government. She asserts that Christians should not compromise with these revolutionary forces, but rather "stand up and say, 'No!'" She also speaks to her prayer partners to work against the possibility of Soviet control because "we would then be at the mercy of Comrade Gorbachev to sell us what we need."

Lindsay's clincher is her daughter-in-law's perception that "we must have a lot more communists in our government and news media than we can imagine."

Personally, I would rather be at the mercy of God to supply my needs while I work for righteousness, rather than ensuring my access of material resources by becoming a partner of the unjust system of apartheid. This biblical view of doing justly escapes these Christian leaders, however, who have allowed the threat of communism (real or imagined) rather than the biblical mandate of mercy and justice to dictate their response to South Africa.

Just as Bosch and Tutu have eloquently appealed, in both their words and lives, for a costly reconciliation that places before the Church the standard of Christ on the cross, so the Church needs to draw on the biblical standard that calls us to seek first the Kingdom of God and His righteousness. Appealing for the protection of the apartheid system because of supposed communist threat and potential inaccessibility to mineral resources valuable to the United States is a clear case of "trusting in chariots and horses" instead of the Lord. Putting Christ's righteousness first would demand that the Church, both in South Africa and abroad, take these reckless, faith-filled steps of trusting God for its own physical well-being while working for the preeminent demands of the Kingdom.

Ultimately, we shouldn't care if the communists also want what black South Africans want. What should motivate us is that justice is what *Jesus* wants, because we take our orders from Him. Justice is what we work for. It's not unthinkable that if the Church stood up and put its life on the line to serve the best interests of the blacks, those revolutionary forces that lean toward Marxist doctrine would lose much of their fire and popular support.

The threat to South Africa today is not communism. Rather it is a Church that has sold its soul for pottage, and models to the world the ugliest of abuses in the name of Jesus Christ. God have mercy!

13
Savages

South Africans will never say, "Look, we've gotten rich in South Africa; we live a comfortable life-style; we intend to keep it that way. Cheap black labor was the key, so cheap black labor has to stay." Instead they offer complicated, convoluted arguments about how blacks are backward thinking, plagued by tribal rivalries and generally childlike and dependent on the guidance and paternalistic care of Big White Brother. The horror of apartheid is served to the blacks on a plate labeled "For your own benefit."

Christians have swallowed whole this myth of black incompetence. Stanley Legg articulates it this way: "The biggest obstacle has yet to be surmounted: how to give full democratic rights to 22 million black people who have lived largely under primitive tribal laws and to whom Western democracy is quite incomprehensible."

Supposedly, the dilemma is quite clear: We would love to give democratic rights to blacks, but they're just not capable of using them responsibly. This assumes that the whites have used their democratic rights responsibly, even though by law they deny the human rights of 73 percent of the population.

These kind of excuses are just a cover-up for the fact that ultimately the South African government has no real plans for an integrated society. It states: "Blacks belong in the homelands created for them, and they have full democratic rights within those boundaries." But if the government sincerely believed blacks are not capable of democracy, it would not have created 10 democratic homelands for them. The truth is that the dream of a comfortable white South Africa simply is not possible if the 73 percent of the population that makes up the slave labor pool were permitted to vote. They would surely change the laws.

One of the clearest propaganda campaigns of the South African government is to assert the unique nature of tribalism, and as a consequence of this, the blacks' incompatibility with white South Africa. But a closer look sheds light on this misleading effort.

In fact, privately the government recognizes the political abilities of blacks like Chief Buthelezi. C.J. Rencken of the Nationalist Party mentioned to me the trouble the government was having in persuading Chief Buthelezi to lead an "independent nation" for the Zulus. Rencken acknowledged that Buthelezi is politically astute, and in fact he manages a political organization with a paid-up constituency twice the size of the Nationalist Party. Rencken doesn't doubt Buthelezi's capability for smooth, orderly participation in the democratic process; he just doesn't want it.

Buthelezi's political organization, Inkatha, has 1.5 million members. Forty percent of them are not Zulu. Buthelezi told me, as he has repeatedly told others, that he believes South Africa should be ruled by a one-man-one-vote system. It's his personal hunch that were such a system employed, he would not be elected president, even though he represents the largest tribe. He believes the electorate would choose Nelson Mandela, the imprisoned leader of the ANC, and were that the case, "I would work under my good friend and brother."

A national poll conducted among blacks in South Africa in 1985 asked simply, "Who would make the best president for South Africa?" Nelson Mandela drew support of 49 percent of those polled; with Bishop Tutu, 24 percent; white liberal Helen Suzman, 11 percent; and Buthelezi, 6 percent following. P.W. Botha, the current president, and Andries Truernicht, a white conservative leader, drew 1 percent each.

No tribal pattern emerges here. In fact, a white woman took more of the vote than Chief Buthelezi. None of the other so-called "tribal chiefs" emerges in this list, in stark contradiction to the government assertion that 10 black tribes would be competing for power.

Political scientists, social scientists and anthropologists around the world agree that in developing countries, "As the cities go, so goes the nation." Tribal villages and rural communities basically follow in the path carved by urban centers. Over half of the blacks in South Africa live in urban centers. Soweto is the most notable example, where over 2 million blacks of every imaginable tribal combination live.

No tribal patterns are discernable among them: Zulus marry Xhosas and their children speak English; Swazis marry Pondos and their children speak English and Zulu. Just as in the United States, where immigrant parents speak their homeland language and their children speak English, so in South Africa's black cities, fourth-generation children don't know what "tribe" their parents' grandparents came from. They speak English, and are bound by a common sense of oppression and destiny that moves them to believe a common, united battle against the white racist system might be the only means to see *their* children live humanely and peacefully. Tribalism is the farthest thought from their minds.

Another argument the South African government uses to establish the need for separate black homelands is its claim that it is unable to find "qualified" blacks to begin a dialogue with that would lead to an integrated democracy.

Legg once again reflects this view of the whites: "President Botha has asked for recommendations from the black community on how this can be done, but very little has been forthcoming. Whites must not appear to prescribe to blacks, but if the black communities are unable to express themselves, how is progress to be made?"

What Legg ignores is that blacks have spoken out, but their agenda for change, namely one-man-one-vote, is not an acceptable starting or ending point for the whites who talk about "dialogue." The black agenda has been clearly stated by leaders ranging from Bishop Tutu, former head of the 12-million member South African Council of Churches, and Nobel Peace Prize winner, to Chief Buthelezi, leader of 6 million Zulus, to Dr. Allan Boesak, former president of the World Alliance of Reformed Churches and founder of the United Democratic Front, which draws together more than 600 black political and labor groups, to Nelson Mandela, who brought together the broadest cross section of South African political leaders in the 1955 congress and is still the most popular black leader, despite more than two decades in prison.

The white government is dismayed that nothing has

been "forthcoming"; no "real leaders" have emerged; indeed the black community has been unable to "express itself." What the government really means is no nationally-recognized black leaders have emerged who are willing to accept the status of "foreigner" and resign themselves to a future in a government-created "independent nation" where their people will live to labor for neighboring white South Africa. Not until those people emerge can there be true "dialogue," say the whites.

The government shows its reluctance to work toward real change by stating that even should a dialogue process begin, no substantial change could be made toward one-man-one-vote for several decades. The system of apartheid took generations to build; surely, it will take as long to dismantle. There must be time to "prepare" blacks for a democratic society where they will be well-schooled not to behave like other savages in the rest of dark Africa.

When white South Africans think of the disastrous consequences of majority rule, they usually cite the example of Zimbabwe. Formerly called Rhodesia, Zimbabwe became a black-run country in 1979. Before then, 250,000 whites had controlled 6 million blacks in a structure not much different than South Africa. The nation stumbled for several years under the change of hands, but today is recognized as giving the blacks a much better life than they had under white leadership. It's been a different story for the whites. The wealth and land they amassed under typical colonial rulership was redistributed to include the disenfranchised black. They necessarily lost their fortunes when a more just system was installed.

Almost half of the whites—most of them British—left the country. They took with them the technological and industrial expertise they had contrólled for generations, and left the blacks holding a bag stripped of the sort of expertise required to operate much of the modern equipment and systems. It took less than five years to restore those functions, and although Zimbabwe will never offer its people the life-style that whites had enjoyed now that the slave pool has been drained, it offers the black majority a vision of hope.

As well as Zimbabwe has done, South Africa has much brighter prospects for an integrated, modern society. The critical difference between South Africa and the other black African states is that the whites aren't colonialists; they have nowhere to go.

Nations like Zimbabwe were exploited by the colonial powers of Britain, France and Portugal. Blacks like Tutu, Boesak and Buthelezi have used the emotional language of "rape" to describe this exploitation, and they're probably using justifiable terminology. The European nations did not ask what could be done for the good of Africa when they conquered its real estate, arbitrarily split up its tribes and territories and established donor republics to meet the demand of the people back home for exotic foods and raw materials for industry. They set up export crops, organized and controlled cheap labor and established transport and communication systems designed only for exporting goods.

When rising nationalism and a changing world attitude toward colonialism in the 1960s forced them to turn these nations over to the people, they simply walked away. The machinery they left in place was not meant to supply the needs of the Africans. Left with that handicap, black governments have been forging ahead toward repairing their battered countries and discovering just forms of government.

South Africa is uniquely prepared to face the challenge of majority rule. The colonial power has become the national power. Dutch farmers who now rule South Africa despise Holland. South Africa is their home. They pursued economic development and technological expertise for the sake of South Africa, not for the benefit of some other country. The wealth generated by the system has stayed within the borders and will continue to do so.

The way that wealth is distributed may well change, though, and this will mean a major adjustment for the whites as they have to live with less luxury. Cheap labor won't be so cheap anymore, so some white families might not be able to afford the ever-present domestic servants. They will have less excess money for certain pleasures and expensive "toys" will dwindle, and work hours for a white population that is used to virtually closing down a city for a week to celebrate Christmas and New Year will increase.

A more just system might mean that blacks will begin to earn enough money to eat, receive medical care, fix the heater in the house for the bitterly cold winter, repair the leaking roof for the summer afternoon rains, install a toilet in the house, purchase a residence where the family can live together and cut back on work hours for the sake of family life.

It's all possible. By God's grace it can all happen. But the transition won't be an easy road if whites remain intransigent.

Although the government and white church leadership ignore the fact, several carefully prepared scenarios have been compiled with the help of the world's leading economists, political scientists and religious leaders to plot smooth transition steps toward a democratic South Africa.

Were the government the least bit interested in such a society, the least it would do is acknowledge those documents and publish a detailed response to the practicality of the suggestions. Instead, it continues to look for qualified blacks who will consult it on how to move forward.

A warning is probably in place: People's patience runs out. Black Africa has been phenomenally forgiving in its treatment of white colonialists who modeled for them the use of brutal military force to accomplish goals. Black revolutions on the whole (save Uganda, whose former leader Idi Amin learned his military tactics from British soldiers) have not come close to reflecting the harsh treatment they received at the hands of Western powers.

The longer one has to wait between *tasting* freedom and *experiencing* it, the more likely a fierce backlash of revenge is in the offing. White South Africa has all the reason in the world to move ahead promptly into a just, integrated society. Black South Africans know that, and one day they might lose their commitment to justice—and a peaceful land—in exchange for retribution and revenge.

That scenario is still unlikely, given the attitude of current black leaders at the helms of the revolutionary movements. By God's grace, South Africa's future will have leaders like Mandela, who says, "All we want is for our children to be free of fear and for their stomachs to be well fed"; and like Bishop Tutu who honestly admits that he would like to hate the whites, but his Lord compels him to love them; and leaders like Chief Buthelezi (my leader by birth), who told me, "Gordon, we cannot judge. We believe against our fears that President Botha is not beyond the reach of Christ, not beyond redemption. So we pray for our oppressors."

14
Wilderness Voices

John the Baptist didn't know the modern rules of public relations. He wore weird clothes, ate the strangest foods and worst of all, never treated public officials with diplomatic respect. Sin was sin, and that's what he called it. He couldn't ignore Herod's adulterous relationship, and though he finally lost his head over that issue, he gained an immeasurable reward.

John wasn't alone as one who stood firm in the truth. The Bible gives us a glimpse of some of his partners: "[They] were tortured and refused to be released, so that they might gain a better resurrection. Some faced jeers and flogging, while still others were chained and put in prison. They were stoned; they were sawed in two; they were put to death by the sword. They went about in sheepskins and goatskins, destitute, persecuted and mistreated . . . . They wandered in deserts and mountains, and in caves and holes in the ground."[1] The Bible tells us the world was not worthy of them.

As I've traveled around South Africa, I've seen glimpses of this kind of person. They are working in faith for a just society that will heal the hurts of the oppressed and bring an end to the defamation of Christ's name. *Their* names might never be known in this world, but their reward is sure as they selflessly serve for a brighter day that they possibly won't experience.

God chooses to make some of those names known to us, and I believe the cross those people carry because of that recognition is the onslaught of hatred, rejection and threats by workers of evil who hate for the Light to shine. These voices of righteousness, these bearers of true love, bring out the ugliest of all beasts and become the targets of those beasts' rage.

They need our prayers. They need our love. But maybe even more, we need their faith.

I'm humbled when I sit with one of these saints and listen to him pour out his love for God and for his country, knowing that love translates into uncomfortable action. I'm convicted when I listen to one of them pray because he's talking to his Daddy, clinging to Him for strength, submitting to Him in the ministry of mercy. The greatest privilege for me in returning to my homeland was to be spurred to a deeper love for my Jesus and a greater no-nonsense daily walk of obedience by the example of these wilderness voices.

Desmond Tutu bears the honor of being the most hated black among white South Africans, but that probably makes him more qualified to speak about love.

"If there's anything about which the Scriptures are clear," says Tutu, "it's that you cannot love God whom you have not seen if you hate your brothers and sisters whom you have seen. The Bible says you're a liar."[2]

Tutu says it's probably easier to be a Christian in South Africa than in other countries because evil is so obvious.

You either live out the gospel's demands in the face of that evil or you don't. Speaking of his training for the Anglican priesthood, he says, "Those men taught me that an authentic Christian spirituality is one where your love for God flows outward, expressing itself in your relationship to your neighbor."

At a large gathering of black and white leaders in late 1985, Bishop Tutu summed up the Christian call to South Africa today in these terms: "Love is the one distinctive characteristic that Jesus said is going to mark us. A transforming love. It's the love of which Jesus also says, 'Greater love has no man than this, that a man should lay down his life for his friends.'[3] And I pray, God, please give us this love. Please give us this love."

Several times since he's prayed that prayer, Tutu has stood in the middle of angry black crowds, mourning the death of another child killed by police bullets, and he's pleaded with them not to retaliate, but to learn the higher way of love. Everytime he does that, he jeopardizes his very life in the hands of a teeming crowd that is losing its patience, that is feeling too much rage to listen to that word *love*.

Nico Smith and his wife Ellen have moved into the black township of Mamelodi to demonstrate that love.

Nico told me the price they pay: "The most difficult part is the fact that your friends turn their backs on you. You become a stranger to your own people, your own family. Many of the family members just never make any contact with me anymore, just as if I'd become a communist or liberal or something. 'Something happened to you; something strange happened to you.' They can't believe that it's because of the gospel that you have changed, that you want to be a faithful servant of Christ the Lord. They all belong to the church, and they've never heard anything like this."

Nico told me that his life really began to change when he told the Lord he'd be willing to obey whatever God would lead him to do. "Daily I live under the knowledge that God is at work in the world and that He calls me to be His co-worker. I don't know what His exact plan is, but I'm open every day. The only thing of which I am definitely convinced in being a co-worker of God is that I must resist evil. I dare not allow Satan to have his way. Wherever I come across injustices or other evils, I must be willing to speak out against them."

Hitler's Germany is a stark reminder to Nico of this theology of resistance. A German woman once told him that during the war she saw a factory not far from her home belch smoke into the air all day long. Only after the war did she discover that was an extermination camp where thousands of Jews were killed.

Nico says, "I believe in our country we're going to have exactly the same thing. That is why I'm trying to put as much of the truth I know about the situation on the table. Many whites hate me for that, but I don't want to allow them to say, 'We didn't know about this.' I think that is one of my main responsibilities as a pastor in the South African situation."

Hundreds of German pastors were imprisoned in Hitler's war for daring to be voices for righteousness. Scores of them were executed. Nico is a student of history and he knows the potential cost. But his history lessons take him back all the way to the cross, and there he learns, "The real meaning of life is to become a servant like Jesus, not to ask what is best for me, but rather how can I serve another person, even if it means death."

My friends Caesar and Chumi Molebatsi smell that death every day, and several times they've come very close to tasting it. Rejected by white Christians who think he's gone liberal, and closely monitored by black radicals ready to "make an example" of him should he collaborate with whites, Caesar walks the tightrope of love in Soweto. He could quit, move to another country and teach theology in a seminary, but he's convinced that Soweto needs to see love in action.

Chumi told me that she literally kisses her kids good-bye every day because she has no assurance she'll see them again. She has reasons to fear: Phone calls have threatened their lives for being "white-lovers." At one time, their son had to stay in hiding while Caesar pled with the radicals for mercy after the boy had broken one of their anti-apartheid rules.

There's no simple formula for Caesar and Chumi to follow as they live out the gospel's love, no security from potential separation, physical afflictions or other hardships. But their standard is the love of Jesus, and every week hundreds of youths in Soweto are growing in their commitment to that same Jesus because they hear the voice and see the life of a prophet, who points them to Jesus.

Michael Cassidy is a different sort of prophetic voice. Born in white Johannesburg in 1936, Cassidy founded African Enterprise in 1962 to bring blacks and whites together to learn love for each other. Black and white clergymen, student and business people come to African Enterprise's center in Pietermaritzburg. Cassidy describes the kind of encounters that take place there:

Perhaps the most touching moment at our center so far was the day when a former prison guard confessed for the first time that he had abused and raped many black women in the course of his assigned duties. In this same gathering were pastors and key church leaders— both black and white.

As he spoke we became aware that one black woman was sobbing uncontrollably. When he finished, the eyes of the group focused on her. Her response was simple and profoundly moving: "I am the one you tortured!"

They were brought together to talk as Christian brother and sister. This led to a Communion service where, from the perspective of the cross of Christ, the two could give and receive forgiveness and could look into each other's eyes again as fellow human beings.

Through African Enterprise, Cassidy sends out multiracial teams to various communities in South Africa where they hold rallies to encourage reconciliation and unity between racial groups. Countless such events have been held and have gone a long way to encourage steps toward reform and understanding on the local level.

In September 1985, Cassidy called together the National Initiative for Reconciliation. Over 400 Christian leaders of all races joined for three days to ask God to renew their resolve to continue in their efforts towards reconciliation. It was there that Bishop Tutu spoke of love, and there that David Bosch explained his understanding of reconciliation. Cassidy is fiercely committed to these gatherings. "Part of our tragedy in South Africa is that we are still prisoners of our histories, not realizing that each group has the key to the other groups' prison."

Cassidy has suffered the ostracism of certain Christian groups who object to his denunciation of the system of apartheid, but he believes that love for one's neighbor will necessarily carry over into political involvement.

"A concern for the political realm is little more than a concern for life," he says. "I don't want to be oppressed. I don't want to be segregated. I don't want my dignity violated. I want to have food to eat. I want clothes on my back. And if that's what I want for myself, then that fruit of the Spirit which is love requires me to covet them for my neighbor. If something political is obstructing my neighbor from getting these things, then I am cast into the political arena. I can't stand in South Africa, preaching the love of Jesus to my black brother, and then without blinking, step with any form of comfort into an apartheid world."

Allan Boesak, a South African colored who was just 38 years old when he was elected president of the 50-million-member World Alliance of Reformed Churches in 1982, explains another reason why the black church leaders have gotten involved in politics: "Our political leaders are not there. They are in exile; they are in jail; they are banned; they've been killed. Who was left?"

Boesak also sees political involvement as a natural consequence of salvation. Believing in Jesus Christ means that "not a single inch of life does not fall under the Lordship of Jesus Christ." It may be art, science, education or politics, but all of life, says Boesak, is accountable to the Lordship of Jesus Christ and "must therefore reflect the demands of this Lord."

His life is no stranger to the hardships that accompany the public prophet. The Afrikaner Resistance Movement (ARM) has singled out both Boesak and Tutu for assassination. Boesak first discovered that fact in a newspaper he was reading as he flew to Johannesburg from Nairobi. He says he has no words to explain the feelings he experienced when his seven-year-old daughter came home crying because she had heard that white people planned to kill him.

Justice will bring freedom to both the oppressed and the oppressor, says Boesak in his book, *Walking on Thorns:*

> If they kill us, it is not because we have picked up a gun. It is not because we hated them, for even now I cannot bring myself to hate those misguided and violent men of the Afrikaner Resistance Movement whose only precious possession in life seems to be their white skin. If they kill us, it is not because we have planned revolution. It will be because we have tried to stand up for justice, because we have refused to accept the cheap "reconciliation" which covers up evil, denies justice, and compromises the God-given dignity of black people. If they kill us, it will be because we love them so much that we refuse to allow them to continue to be our oppressors.[4]

Early in 1985, Boesak experienced another form of persecution: slander. Police-generated rumors spread, accusing him of having an affair with his secretary. Several white church leaders appealed to him to step down from his church posts because he was denegrating the name of Christ. Boesak's justice ministry looked surely doomed.

Boesak defended himself vehemently. He spoke out

against the accusations, which he saw as another sign of "the utterly sick society in which we live. Even the church has been used to further the aims of this smear campaign."

The rumor caused such uproar that eventually the parliament asked the Minister of Law and Order to explain the smear campaign. He had to admit that the only evidence he held was the fact that Boesak and the secretary had been seen meeting "at various hotels." Boesak was eventually cleared of the charges.

Boesak says he wouldn't be jeopardizing himself or his family "if I didn't believe in Jesus Christ as my personal Saviour." It's not easy for him, but because of Jesus in him, he's discovered that he would much rather be disobedient to the South African government than to be disobedient to God.

In a controversial action during 1985, Boesak called for the Church of South Africa to pray for the downfall of the white government. He wasn't appealing for revolution or bloodshed, simply that somehow, by the mercy of God, that government would collapse and be replaced by more just rulers.

White churches protested with outrage at this call, and were convinced that this sealed the fact that Boesak was really a Marxist-liberal who should be locked up. Those same screaming churches went to the battlefield during World War II to overthrow the government of Hitler. They applauded the courage of people like Bonhoeffer who laid his life on the line by joining an assassination plot against Hitler. Surely these Christians prayed for Hitler's supernatural downfall to prevent the need for going to battle with guns.

People like Boesak don't see apartheid as very different from Hitler's Germany, and there's good reason to feel that way. Probably as many as 2 million black children have died directly because of the apartheid system during the past three decades.

Yet Boesak, Bosch, Tutu, Cassidy, Smith and Molebatsi don't see the answer in violence. They've all seen the ugliness of violence, and they're absolutely opposed to it. In the entry way to Boesak's office hangs a poster with a black and white hugging each other. Superimposed on their hug are the words, "A modest proposal for peace: Let the Christians of the world agree that they will not kill each other."

Nowhere else, except perhaps in Northern Ireland, could these words make more sense. Nowhere else is the message of the cross more desperately needed for the world to witness that Christians don't kill each other; rather they die for one another. These prophets, these voices in the wilderness, are carrying death within themselves daily. They've counted the cost of reconciliation and they're paying that cost because they love Jesus dearly. The world is not worthy of them, but just maybe, by God's grace, that torn up part of the world that is South Africa will be saved because of them.

Notes
1. Hebrews 11:35-38.
2. See 1 John 4:20.
3. See John 15:13.
4. Allan Boesak, *Walking On Thorns,* copyright © 1984 World Council of Churches, used by permission of Wm. B. Eerdmans Publishing Co.

15
Uncle Sam

The agony of South Africa has captured the sympathies of many Americans. Recalling our racial struggles of the 1950s and 1960s, many Americans want to work to see justice established in South Africa. Student groups and local governments have pressed for American companies doing business in South Africa to treat their black employees fairly, or withdraw their economic support for the system.

Divestment is their rallying cry. Their claim is that Americans who make a profit in South Africa do so at the expense of the oppressed blacks. Ending our economic involvement in apartheid would not only cleanse our complicitous guilt, it might even force the government to make real changes.

Without question the United States has an enormous economic interest in South Africa. U.S. companies own half of South Africa's car and tire industries and supply most of the country's computers; the United States is the largest foreign financial investor (investments increased from $1.5 billion in 1976 to $14 billion in 1985); and American companies employ 1 percent of the black population.

People on both continents debate the merits of divestment and of official sanctions that the U.S. government could impose to keep U.S. businesses out of South Africa.

U.S. Ambassador Designate J. Douglas Holladay is a Christian. He believes that the system of apartheid is unethical and that Christian justice ultimately demands the dismantling of that system. But economic sanctions don't present themselves to Holladay as a means to influence the South African government toward change, because "sanctions historically have been slow to act and not very effective."

Advocates of sanctions, however, point to Zimbabwe-Rhodesia as a case where sanctions did prove effective. In the late 1970s, Rhodesia's white government reeled under international economic sanctions. Ultimately the white rulers had to throw in the towel because with a truncated economy, they couldn't afford the expense of mobilizing the military to maintain control over black revolutionaries.

During late 1985, President Reagan imposed very limited sanctions on South Africa, and the effects were almost immediate. The country halted production of the Krugerrand (a popular gold coin that was a major source of revenue for South Africa); seven white labor organizations hurriedly met with the outlawed ANC to discuss a possible solution and by early 1986, 14 businesses were going bankrupt every day. President Botha, in a first for his party, had to freeze foreign-debt payments and negotiate a more manageable payment schedule.

It is probably still too soon to tell whether these limited sanctions have actually brought about changes in the Botha Administration policies. Botha's *rhetoric* about dismantling apartheid has increased significantly, even to the disclosure of some surprising plans for Natal, the most progressive of South Africa's four provinces and home of Chief Buthelezi. The experiment would involve a joint black and white administrative body and, in effect, two governors (Buthelezi would be one of them), who would both hold veto power. Whether they will be permitted to change Natal structurally by abolishing all racial discrimination is not yet known. Currently, provincial governments do not have the power to overturn national apartheid laws.

Buthelezi is willing to give it a go. He feels it's a constructive step forward and a necessary part of the negotiating process. He hopes that blacks will be given enough legislative say to demonstrate their capability of coexisting peacefully with whites.

Allan Boesak and Desmond Tutu reject the Natal plan, however, and view it as simply a sophisticated version of the homeland concept. Blacks will feel like they have power, but will still be ultimately controlled by Big White Brother. Winnie Mandela, wife of the imprisoned ANC leader, showed her response in May by leading the nation's largest black boycott in history. More than 1.5 million black laborers stayed away from work, and 1 million students stayed away from school to show their solidarity.

Botha himself protests strongly against the idea of complete sanctions, basing his argument, strangely enough, on humanitarian reasons. He claims sanctions would be damaging to the blacks who already live on the breadline! Blacks find it laughable that he would suddenly express solidarity with their hardships when all their suffering is the direct consequence of President Botha's party.

Elijah Barayi, president of the newly formed Congress of South African Trade Unions says that divestment might be the only answer for peaceful transition. His organization already has 450,000 members, representing 34 black labor unions.

The Reagan Administration has picked up President Botha's protest and used it as its major rationale to not proceed with full sanctions. Ambassador Holladay told me that the Administration's policy is to avoid anything that would "destabilize a country that is economically providing jobs and increasing opportunities for blacks over there."

The effectiveness of sanctions may be debatable, but the idea that Botha's government is "increasing opportunities for blacks" is a complete misreading of the black experience of increasing police and military control, continued forced relocations and higher death rates.

Opponents of total divestment fear that it would spell economic ruin for well-developed businesses and ultimately complete poverty for all of South Africa's residents. Desmond Tutu, on the other hand, sees it as the quickest, least painful way to pin the white administration to the conference table for legitimate dialogue with respected black leaders. Tutu says that it's fully within black interests that the long-range economic stability of the nation remain intact so that all South African citizens, black and white, can enjoy its benefits.

Tutu's call for immediate sanctions against his nation is in itself a dangerous act, because publicly supporting economic sanctions is a crime listed as "treason" by the government, a crime that could carry life imprisonment or even the death penalty. Tutu's international prominence as a Nobel laureate no doubt saves him from those consequences.

Tutu has influenced 15 U.S. corporations to join the crusade for complete divestment. They are: Perkins-

Elmer Corp. (scientific instruments); Oak Industries (electrical equipment); City Investing Company; West Point-Pepperell (fabrics); Bluebell (jeans); Pan Am; International Harvester; Ecolaire Company; PepsiCo; Smith International (mining equipment); Kidwell (mobile homes); Helena Rubinstein; BBD&O (advertising); Phibro-Solomon (securities and commodities); and Apple.

Tutu's ministry constantly has him mixing with the ordinary black urban laborer, and qualifies him to speak on this issue. Every week he conducts funerals for blacks killed in police violence; every week he has to console mothers who have lost yet another child to the harsh system; every week he puts his life on the line in the middle of desperate, angry mobs that are on the edge of exploding with rage like a closed can of boiling water. Tutu's daily experience is that of ministering to people whose hardships have only increased and whose despair is turning into a hatred that could erupt into the most violent of backlashes yet.

Uncle Sam is not very popular among black South Africans, and Ambassador Holladay acknowledges that fact. "It's a hard role we're in," he told me. "We're trying to keep diplomatic avenues open with the South African government and use our influence. We could cut off our tie and have great credibility with the black community, but we feel we can make a difference by staying involved. Some people aren't going to understand that."

Actually, the situation is that people *are* going to understand that. Black South Africans who have become well acquainted with the double-talk of their own government are quick to perceive this double-talk of the Reagan Administration.

In May 1986, the United States launched a military

expedition against neighboring black-run Angola. Working through the CIA, the United States used Namibia as its base of operation (Namibia, or South West Africa, is controlled by South Africa) and channeled $15 million through UNITA, the South African-based terrorist organization currently at work to overthrow the Angolan government. Reagan has publicly stated, "We want to be very helpful to what Dr. Savimbi [military leader of UNITA] and his people are trying to do."

Black South Africans look on as Reagan and Botha join hands to overthrow the black government in Angola with military force, and their resentment rises because President Reagan has refused simply to *talk* publicly with black ANC leaders in South Africa, because it's "against the Administration's foreign policy to cooperate with any violent movements."

Such double-talk exasperates blacks in South Africa, and consequently, anti-U.S. sentiment is at an all-time high. The United States literally faces the prospect of an anti-U.S. government in South Africa one day. As Tutu says, "The American government has an amazing talent to back the wrong horse."

Understandably, black leaders feel Reagan's foreign policy is racially loaded. They have lived under the control of whites who simply treat blacks as a means to their own economic ends and enjoyment, and Reagan is being perceived as simply another one of those colonial powers who does not ask, "What is good for the people of that land?" but rather, "How can our nation benefit from the resources in that land?"

It's a sad commentary on the U.S. government, which claims to operate from Christian principles. In the words of Ambassador Holladay, as he explained U.S. policy to me, "Our goal is to enlarge the world of morality and justice in ever-increasing ways, so that the people of God can find opportunities to really bring the mind of Christ to bear upon every level of society."

I sense that Holladay is sincere in that statement, even though I do not agree with the foreign policy that directs his work.

Black South Africa is beginning to think that Uncle Sam looks a lot like their white God. That's a damaging blow to the gospel.

16
Cross Roads

American Christians probably all agree that apartheid is a blight. Unfortunately, there are many Christians like Ambassador Holladay whose sincere interest in working toward a solution in South Africa is strangled by a misguided understanding of the country's problems.

It didn't surprise me that when I asked Nico Smith what American Christians could do to help South Africa, he responded, "Go learn servanthood." Nico has seen enough Christians from the United States go blundering through the country like a bull elephant recklessly smashing its way through the forest.

These Christians, who sincerely want to see the gospel move forward, are blinded by their own Western handicap, which instead of making them servants when they become Christians, made them rulers. Nico sees white South African lordship over blacks as simply a mirror image of the Western identity of being "rulers; superior, self-assured and strong rulers, not servants."

But more than their superiority, these Christians carry American political baggage that blinds them to the real issues in South Africa. Consequently, like the elephant, they trample on huts instead of fires because their own blinders keep them from seeing things as they really are.

Jerry Falwell has not been good for South Africa. In his worldview, Christians must hold to a pro-American, anti-communist bias; as a result he makes pronouncements about South Africa that are an offense to the gospel of Jesus Christ. They are also, as one columnist has stated, an offense to "Americans who still believe that 'liberty and justice for all' is an ideal worth pursuing." He has branded Christians who work tirelessly for the Kingdom in South Africa out of their love for and obedience to Jesus as communist dupes working for Soviet world domination.

Falwell stormed through South Africa for one week of his life and claims that he had consulted people "in every segment of every community" in South Africa and is thus qualified to speak forth the solution. And he went a step further, denouncing Tutu as a phony because he "purports to speak for South African blacks." Falwell had no hesitation in assuming the role of mouthpiece for the black South Africans.

His position on South Africa is simply incompatible with the demands of the gospel of Jesus. When he looks at South Africa, all Falwell sees is the "threat" of communism; he doesn't see the outrage of millions of blacks denied justice and even the most basic human rights. The gospel's demands to feed the hungry and comfort the oppressed hardly show up in his pronouncements on South Africa. He has exchanged the Christian response to the suffering of 22 million people for a strident call that appears to back their oppressors. This response has further damaged the reputation of Jesus among blacks in that land, as well as among thousands of blacks in the States who still suspect that much of the American gospel is a white theology.

Had Falwell not been so vocal in his ill-founded anti-communist crusade, and had he not had such a profound influence on much of the Christian mind-set in the United States, it would not have been necessary to call him on the carpet.* Several other U.S.-based Christian ministries have blundered through South Africa with their in-control mind-sets and anti-communist blinders, but their influence isn't great enough in the United States to justify the mention of their names. They raise hundreds of thousands of dollars for their ministries by pulling the emotional "godless-communism" strings of their donors' money purses instead of equipping them with a biblical standard for pursuing justice. Their newsletters chronicle the accounts of black Christians suffering because of communist-inspired radicals who are behind all of South Africa's unrest. Communists, they claim, and not the apartheid system, are the real cause of persecution in that nation.

God save South Africa from those rogues!

Working for the true gospel in South Africa requires a balance between our determination to see change and our realization that change may not come as we expect. Graham Beggs, a white South African, has been learning to walk that balance. As he drove me through the back hills of Zululand, showing me the community development pro-

---

*Name-calling is a particular sickness in the American church today, and so it's with much reservation that I've referred to Falwell's unfortunate blundering. I've been in contact with his office several times in the course of writing this manuscript in order to maintain an open channel for dialogue and communication, and although Mr. Falwell has been unable to meet with me personally to discuss the issues of this book he agreed at my request to have the manuscript sent to his office for review before it went to press to give him adequate opportunity for rebuttal.

jects he was involved in, Graham related a personal lesson: "I remember an occasion when I saw little black children huddled together at a gas station to protect themselves from the pouring rain. A group of white roughs drove up and sprayed these little children from the water faucet. It was a bitterly cold day. I didn't like what I saw and thought it needed to be put right. I took a watering can for filling radiators, and I let these guys have it. They overpowered me, and they let me have it. That day I learned to recognize that political force is exactly the same. It's man taking an implement into his own hand. Politics is part of our life here on earth, but the name of Jesus is the name to call upon that is greater than the name of politics."

Calling on the name of Jesus is a costly proposition, because the sword of truth is a double-edged implement. As we swing it to cut through the injustices of society, it also swings back and cuts into our own hearts, demanding a deeper level of submission to Christ's Lordship in our lives.

Those of us American Christians who want to serve South Africa stand at a crossroad that will point us down the "Cross Road." There we will have to crucify our own American nationalism that wants to look at South Africa through its own grid. On that road, we'll have to endure the sometimes painful journey of carrying the cross; we'll have to put the needs of South Africans above the interests of the wealthy United States. We'll discover that serving others means putting God and the world before our country. But we'll receive a new freedom on that road—a freedom to abandon ourselves to the priority of "Christ's Kingdom first."

We'll also find ourselves carrying a much deeper love

for our own nation than we'd ever imagined, because as we give of our love to others, God gives us back a love for our own. And it will be an authentic love—not one that takes its cues from political paradigms, but one that is rooted in the love of God Almighty Himself, a love weak in the eyes of the world, but powerful in the might of the Spirit.

There is a place for this kind of American love-servant in South Africa.

First, we need to pray for South African Christians that they will develop that same servant heart. Nico Smith says that it's the mercy of God that blacks know how to be servants. "I see white people scorn them, shout at them, and hit them, but they just carry on. They have an unbelievable gift of tolerance." Whites need to learn of that transforming nature of the gospel that makes us servants of one another.

Pray for those prophets who work tirelessly for the sake of the King. Pray for the mothers and daughters who suffer abuses of their dignity and pray for the children who fear for their daddies who speak up.

Give money (a resource appendix at the end of the book lists all sorts of opportunities). Many black Christian leaders need the selfless support of Christians who will go beyond the "control" sort of giving that can often come from white churches (where most of South Africa's ministry money resides). Blacks need scholarship money to advance their theological and technical training. Some pastors need to hire lawyers to defend their religious freedoms; others need to get away to a place of retreat for refreshment. The Mennonite Central Committee is particularly active in these two.

Send your support to Bread for the World (a Christian

lobbying group in Washington, D.C.) earmarked for influencing U.S. legislation to care for the hungry in South Africa who starve because of apartheid.

Speak up. Don't allow the gospel to continue receiving the abuse it has because of the Church's silence. Contact your denominational headquarters to see if a formal letter of protest can be sent to President Botha. The following excerpt is from a letter sent by the Baptist World Alliance (membership 34 million), which expressed concern about "indiscriminate arrests, imprisonment and persecution of black South Africans seeking their just rights under God":

> We abhor and denounce apartheid and its demonic system, including forceable relocation of black populations and destruction of their homes by bulldozing; humiliating discrimination in many public places with rigid pass laws; arbitrary arrest and detention indefinitely without trial; and the disenfranchisement of the black majority.
>
> We Baptists join with Christians of South Africa and the world in praying for a peaceful solution to the tragedy that confronts your country. We call upon all men and women of good will to work constructively for the dismantling of apartheid and for a democratic system of government.
>
> Mr. President, the hour is late; you must act now to avoid further bloodshed. In the name of God, please seize the opportunity to work for the freedom of all people in South Africa.

Similar letters could be sent to leaders of white

churches in South Africa. Nico Smith says we need to keep asking the South African Church questions: "Are you sure you're doing God's will in that country? Are you fulfilling your prophetic calling? Are you sure the gospel you are believing is really the gospel of Jesus Christ?" He wishes more Christians had asked German Christians these questions during Hitler's reign.

A Churches' Emergency Committee on South Africa has been formed by the leadership of the Presbyterian Church, the United Methodist Church, the Episcopal Church, several Lutheran denominations, the Southern Baptists, the African Methodist Episcopal Church, the Greek Orthodox Archdiocese and the Roman Catholic Church. They've agreed to press for government economic sanctions, divestment of U.S. holdings, boycotts against American companies that refuse to divest and the end of continued bank credit for the South African government. Write them for information about their campaign.

If you're a student, speak up on your college campus. Too often secular groups are leading the way in justice concerns. Be a witness to the justice heart of Jesus and the integrity of the gospel. If you attend a Christian college, rattle the cage.

Some Christians could serve directly in South Africa. Forging linkages between black and white congregations in South Africa will go a long way toward encouraging the downtrodden blacks not to grow weary, and the fearful whites to let go of the security that apartheid affords them. White Americans *serving under* black South African leadership will model a message desperately needed in that land.

South Africa offers the Church worldwide the opportunity to discover anew the costly discipleship that Christ

calls us to. The South African tragedy is a searing indict-
ment of cheap Christianity. It reveals the damages that
result when the Church sells its soul in exchange for the
world's goods. Apartheid may be the occasion the worldwide Church of Jesus Christ so badly needs to reestablish
its all-consuming, loving, merciful, demanding heritage of
the cross. American Christians can be a vital part in that
step forward.

Who knows, it may be this sort of daily dying on the
cross road that could give South Africa the privilege of
leading the rest of the Church into a renewed passion for
the Kingdom to be known all over the earth "as the waters
cover the sea."[1]

The apostle Paul led the religious community in his day
to kill off those Christians who were, in his mind, compro-
mising the purity of the nation and beliefs of the Jews. Yet,
after his dramatic conversion, he blazed the path of mercy
that led the Church in its global mission to extend the love
and justice of Jesus Christ to all the nations of the world. In
the curious dealings of God, the one most despised by
Christians became the one most qualified to teach them.

Perhaps this curious honor awaits the white persecutors in South Africa.

Note
1. Habakkuk 2:14.

17
Dayspring

Hope.

It's an illogical gift that defies facts, that returns resolve for fear, patience for despair and belief for bitterness.

Hope looks evil in the eye and laughs at the beast as it shrinks into a toothless termite at the foot of the cross. Hope is a gift that knows the day will come when the Victor who has already conquered the evil one will come forward to gather His very own under His protective hand.

Hope is the uncanny future of South Africa. The injustices are undeniable. The government's intention to stay white and powerful is unquestionable. Yet Christian hope, while working tirelessly for love and justice, looks forward to the surprising blow to midnight, the crushing of darkness and the unexpected arrival of day.

Christian hope does not seek retribution. Rather it longingly waits for the privilege of embracing a wayward prodigal that has come home. It dresses him up with the finest of garb, forgives him of all wrongdoing and invites him to a party for all who love the Father.

God has blessed South Africa with some unusual black Christian leaders who speak for the whole nation of blacks oppressed by the white Church. Within their chests are hearts that have become tender in the face of oppression, rather than hard. Their spirit of forgiveness increases with every new act of violence because they follow the model of their crucified Lord who asked that His persecutors be forgiven as He hung in public view, awaiting His slow, certain death.

Chief Buthelezi told me, "We must not destroy this country with hate. That is not God's will."

Bishop Tutu says that God has given them an extraordinary country. "You pray with a black man whose home is to be demolished by government authorities the next day, whose wife and children will be moved to some place he does not know, and yet he prays, 'God, thank you for loving us.' You speak to a brother who has just been released from prison where he has undergone third-degree torture. Instead of bitterness coming out of him, he prays for his tormentors because they are 'God's children behaving like animals.'"

The night is nearly over in South Africa. That is our daily hope against hope. That is our prayer for a stubborn people. That is our heart's cry for the sake of Christ's name, so abused in this country. That is our confidence— the Morning Star is about to sparkle through the darkness.

The Freedom Charter

The Freedom Charter was unanimously adopted by the largest gathering of black leadership in South African history, the "Congress of the People," in 1955. It remains the clearest statement of black aspirations for the future of their country.

We, the people of South Africa, declare for all our country and the world to know:

—that South Africa belongs to all who live in it, black and white, and that no government can justly claim authority unless it is based on the will of all the people;

—that our people have been robbed of their birthright to land, liberty and peace by a form of government founded on injustice and inequality;
—that our country will never be prosperous or free until all our people live in brotherhood, enjoying equal rights and opportunities;
—that only a democratic state, based on the will of all the people, can secure to all their birthright without distinction of colour, race, sex or belief;
And therefore, we the people of South Africa, black and white together—equals, countrymen and brothers—adopt this Freedom Charter. And we pledge ourselves to strive together, sparing neither strength nor courage, until the democratic changes set out here have been won.

The people shall govern!

Every man and woman shall have the right to vote for and to stand as a candidate for all bodies which make laws;

All people shall be entitled to take part in the administration of the country;

The rights of the people shall be the same, regardless of race, colour or sex;

All bodies of minority-rule, advisory boards, councils and authorities shall be replaced by democratic organs of self-government.

All national groups shall have equal rights!

There shall be equal status in the bodies of state, in the courts and in the schools for all national groups and races;

All people shall have equal right to use their own languages, and to develop their own folk culture and customs;

All national groups shall be protected by law against insults to their race and national pride;

The preaching and practice of national, race or colour discrimination and contempt shall be a punishable crime;

All apartheid laws and practices shall be set aside.

The people shall share in the country's wealth!

The national wealth of our country, the heritage of all South Africans, shall be restored to the people;

The mineral wealth beneath the soil, the banks and monopoly industry shall be transferred to the ownership of the people as a whole;

All other industry and trade shall be controlled to assist the well-being of the people;

All people shall have equal rights to trade where they choose, to manufacture and to enter all trades, crafts and professions.

The land shall be shared among those who work it!

Restriction of land ownership on a racial basis shall be ended, and all the land redivided amongst those who work it, to banish famine and land hunger;

The state shall help the peasants with implements, seed, tractors and dams to save the soil and assist the tillers.

Freedom of movement shall be guaranteed to all who work on the land;

All shall have the right to occupy land wherever they choose;

People shall not be robbed of their cattle, and forced labour and farm prisons shall be abolished.

All shall be equal before the law!

No one shall be imprisoned, deported or restricted without a fair trial;

No one shall be condemned by the order of any government official;

The courts shall be representative of all people;

Imprisonment shall be only for serious crimes against the people, and shall aim at re-education, not vengeance;

The police force and army shall be open to all on an equal basis and shall be the helpers and protectors of the people;

All laws which discriminate on grounds of races, colour or belief shall be repealed.

All shall enjoy human rights!

The law shall guarantee to all their rights to speak, to organise, to meet together, to punish, to preach, to worship and to educate their children;

The privacy of the house from police raids shall be protected by law;

All shall be free to travel without restriction from countryside to town, from province to province and from South Africa abroad;

Pass Laws, permits, and all other laws restricting these freedoms, shall be abolished.

There shall be work and security!

All who work shall be free to form unions, to elect their officers and to make wage agreements with their employers;

The state shall recognise the right and duty of all to work, and to draw full unemployment benefits;

Men and women of all races shall receive equal pay for equal work;

There shall be a forty-hour working week, a national minimum wage, paid annual leave, and sick leave for all workers, and maternity leave on full pay for all working mothers;

Miners, domestic workers, farm workers, and civil servants shall have the same rights as all others who work;

Child labour, compound labour, the tot system and contract labour shall be abolished.

The doors of learning and of culture shall be opened!

The government shall discover, develop and encourage national talent for the enhancement of our cultural life;

All the cultural treasures of mankind shall be open to all, by free exchange of books, ideas and contact with other lands;

The aim of education shall be to teach the youth to love their people and their culture, to honour human brotherhood, liberty and peace;

Education shall be free, compulsory, universal and equal for all children;

Higher education and technical training shall be opened to all by means of state allowances and scholarships awarded on the basis of merit;

Adult illiteracy shall be ended by a mass state education plan;

Teachers shall have all the rights of other citizens;

The colour bar in cultural life, in sports and in education shall be abolished.

There shall be houses, security and comfort!

All people shall have the rights to live where they choose, to be decently housed, and to bring up their families in comfort, and security;

Unused housing space shall be made available to the people;

Rent and prices shall be lowered, food plentiful and no one shall go hungry;

A preventive health scheme shall be run by the state;

Free medical care and hospitalisation shall be provided for all, with special care for mothers and young children;

Slums shall be demolished, and new suburbs built where all have transport, roads, lighting, playing fields, crèches and social centres;

The aged, the orphans, the disabled and the sick shall be cared for by the state;

Rest, leisure and recreation shall be the right of all;

Fenced locations and ghettoes shall be abolished, and laws which break up families shall be repealed;

South Africa shall be a fully independent state, which respects the rights and sovereignty of nations.

There shall be peace and friendship!

South Africa shall strive to maintain world peace and the settlement of all international disputes by negotiation—not war.

Peace and friendship amongst all our people shall be secured by upholding the equal rights, opportunities and status of all;

The people of the protectorates—Basutoland [Lesotho], Bechuanaland [Botswana] and Swaziland—shall be free to decide for themselves their own future;

The rights of all the people of Africa to independence

and self-government shall be recognised, and shall be the basis of close cooperation;

Let all who love their people and their country now say, as we say here:

"These freedoms we will fight for, side by side, throughout our lives, until we have won our liberty."

APPENDIX 2
Join South Africa's Struggles

I. Books

Read more about the situation in South Africa, its history, its heroes. Get to know the personal perspectives and biblical hope of Desmond Tutu and Allan Boesak through their books:

Tutu, Desmond. *Crying in the Wilderness: The Struggle for Justice in South Africa.* Grand Rapids, MI: William B. Eerdmans Publishing Co., 1982.

———. *Hope and Suffering.* Grand Rapids, MI: William B. Eerdmans Publishing Co., 1984.

Boesak, Allan. *Walking on Thorns: The Call to Chris-*

tian Obedience. Grand Rapids, MI: William B. Eerdmans Publishing Co., 1984.

Dig into the theological underpinnings of apartheid:

DeGruchy, John W. and Charles Villa-Vicencio, eds. *Apartheid Is a Heresy.* Grand Rapids, MI: William B. Eerdmans Publishing Co., 1983.

DeGruchy, John W. *Bonhoeffer and South Africa Today.* Grand Rapids, MI: William B. Eerdmans, 1984.

Read secular books on South Africa's history, situation and U.S. relations:

Lelyveld, Joseph. *Move Your Shadow.* New York: Times Books, 1985. A Pulitzer prize-winning account of apartheid's impact on lives in South Africa.

Danaher, Kevin. *In Whose Interest: A Guide to U.S.- South Africa Relations.* Washington, DC: Institute for Policy Studies, 1984. Well-researched, yet brief analysis of U.S. policy toward South Africa.

Read books on the biblical mandate for Christians to be involved in justice:

Stott, John. *Involvement: Being a Responsible Christian in a Non-Christian Society.* Old Tappan, NJ: Fleming H. Revell Co., 1984. Looks at biblical and historical reasons for getting involved, as well as particular issues.

Perkins, John. *With Justice for All.* Ventura, CA: Regal Books, 1982.
———. *Let Justice Roll Down.* Ventura, CA: Regal Books, 1976.

Both deal with justice issues based on Perkins' experience of establishing a community development ministry for blacks in Mississippi.

Waldron, Scott. *Bring Forth Justice.* Grand Rapids, MI: William B. Eerdmans Publishing Co., 1980. An exploration of the biblical themes of mission, discipleship and injustice.

Sider, Ronald. *Rich Christians in an Age of Hunger.* Downers Grove, IL: InterVarsity Press, 1985. An examination of world hunger issues with a strong biblical analysis of Christian concerns for justice.

Krass, Alfred C. *Pastoring for Peace and Justice.* The Other Side, 300 W. Apsley St., Philadelphia, PA 19144, 1986. A booklet for pastors who want to lead their churches in a concern for justice.

II. Organizations

There are a multitude of organizations involved in various aspects of the struggle for justice in South Africa. Some of these are specifically church-related; others are not. Some aggressively pursue economic and political strategies aimed at forcing change in South Africa by influencing U.S. businesses and government. Others focus on providing information and educational resources. They are included here as sources of information on apartheid and the anti-apartheid movement, as well as places to get involved in the political process.

Africa News
P.O. Box 3857
Durham, NC 27702

A bi-weekly newsletter on Africa in general, frequently deals with events in South Africa. Subscription $30/year.

American Committee on Africa/Africa Fund
198 Broadway
New York, NY 10038
212/962-1210

Researches and publishes information on South Africa, including the "South Africa Fact Sheet," a statistical summary of the impact of apartheid on the lives of blacks.

American Friends Service Committee
Peace Education Division, Southern Africa
    Program
1501 Cherry Street
Philadelphia, PA 19102
215/241-7169

Building a constituency in the United States in support of freedom and justice in South Africa, provides literature and films. Publishes the "U.S. Anti-Apartheid Newsletter" (quarterly, $10/year), which tracks action around the country, including that of church groups.

Amnesty International
1 Easten St.
London WC1X 8DJ
United Kingdom

International watchdog organization tracks human rights violations by governments around the world, including South Africa. Publishes an annual report and newsletters. Coordinates letter-writing campaigns on behalf of political prisoners.

Bread for the World
802 Rhode Island Ave. NE
Washington, DC 20018
202/269-0200

A Christian antihunger advocacy group, supports sanctions against South Africa in order to end apartheid and the related problems of hunger in South Africa. Members receive a monthly newsletter describing current legislation and quarterly publications that deal with issues in more depth (membership $25/year).

Evangelicals for Social Action
712 G. Street SE
Washington, DC 20003
202/543-5330

A loosely structured network of local chapters that provides educational material on biblical justice and resources for action on the local level. Publishes newsletters on a variety of peace and justice issues. Can help you start a local chapter in your church or campus to educate Christians on justice, meet a local need, or get involved in anti-apartheid activities.

**Interfaith Center for Corporate
    Responsibility**
475 Riverside Dr., Room 566
New York, NY 10115
212/870-2294

Coalition of Roman Catholic and Protestant churches, coordinates research, shareholder resolutions, and divestment activities to put economic pressure on South Africa.

International Defense and Aid Fund
P.O. Box 17
Cambridge, MA 02138
617/491-8343

An international humanitarian organization based in London, raises money for legal defense of political prisoners and help for their families. Also publishes books, newsletters and photo exhibits.

TransAfrica
545 8th St. SE
Washington, DC 20003
202/547-2550

Lobby for Africa and Caribbean that deals frequently with South African issues (membership $12.50/year). Also publishes journal and issue briefs (subscription $20/year).

United Nations Centre Against Apartheid
UN Secretariat
New York, NY 10017
212/754-6674

Publishes free studies on all aspects of apartheid and the anti-apartheid movement.

Washington Office on Africa
110 Maryland Ave. NE
Washington, DC 20002
202/546-7961

A church- and union-sponsored lobbying organization.

Publishes "Washington Notes on Africa" (quarterly, $15/ year), which follows the anti-apartheid movement in the United States and South Africa, and other educational materials. Sponsors the "Africa Hotline," a 24-hour telephone service with updates on legislation bearing on apartheid: 202/546-0408.

III. Mission Agencies

Serve the cause of justice in South Africa by supporting, or even joining, Christians who are living out the gospel's demands. If possible, ask that your funds go to support black Christian workers' churches, which often lack the resources to support them.

Africa Co-operative Action Trust (ACAT)
P.O. Box 1743
Pietermaritzburg 3200
South Africa

ACAT, a Pentecostal group, works throughout Southern Africa in rural development, education and training. In South Africa, they work in several of the homelands, helping the most impoverished people work together to produce more food, safe water and handcraft industries. Evangelism is also an integral part of their work.

African Enterprise
P.O. Box 908
Pasadena, CA 91102
818/796-5830

African Enterprise works for racial reconciliation

through multi-racial teams and its Center for Leadership Training in Pietermaritzburg (see chapter 14 for more information). Write them for prayer letters, to support a South African Christian or to serve an internship with them. AE has also played a key role in the National Initiative for Reconciliation. Follow this movement by writing for their newsletter:

NIR Process News
P.O. Box 647
Pietermaritzburg 3200
South Africa

Christian Nationals Evangelism Commission (CNEC)
P.O. Box 15025
San Jose, CA 95115-0025
408/298-0965

CNEC supports the work of several black and colored ministries in South Africa, including Youth Alive, which Caesar Molebatsi directs (see chapter 1), and the Bible Band, a ministry for colored youth in Cape Town. Support one of these ministries, or contact CNEC for ways you could go to South Africa and serve under one of them.

Mennonite Central Committee (MCC)
Box M
Akron, PA 17901
717/859-1151

MCC has two unique programs in South Africa. Their *Crisis Fund* provides emergency assistance for people who have been detained by the police, had their houses burned or are otherwise suffering because of South Africa's struggles. Their *Servanthood Sabbaticals* give Christian workers the opportunity to come to the United States for a period of rest and renewal so they can continue to minister in that difficult situation.

IV. Write Letters

Christians need to speak up about their convictions on South Africa. Write your Senator or Congressman, urging him or her to vote for bills that will help the majority of South Africa's people. Bread for the World or The Africa Hotline can help you stay informed as these issues arise (see above). Write government officials in the U.S. and South Africa, urging them to work toward the end of apartheid.

> Ambassador J. Douglas Holladay
> Department of State
> SAWG Room 3243
> Washington, DC 20520

> President of the Republic of South Africa
> Mr. P.W. Botha
> The Marks Building
> Cape Town
> South Africa

> General J. Coetzee
> Commissioner of Police
> Private Bag X302
> Pretoria 0001
> South Africa

General Coetzee is responsible for political prisoners and those detained without trial or legal counsel.

V. Prayer

Contact Evangelicals for Social Action for a monthly prayer letter to help you in your fellowship or personal prayer times in your commitment to South Africa.

> **Intercessors for Peace and Freedom: South Africa**
> 712 G Street, S.E.
> Washington, DC 20003
> 202/543-5330